Grace in Chaos

BIBLICAL HOPE FOR THE HARD DAYS OF MOTHERHOOD

This study belongs to:

_____

_____

KRISTYN PEREZ

"Our goal is not to be perfect moms but simply to point to the perfect Savior."

In this study

BEFORE YOU BEGIN

Study Suggestions	6	Timeline of Scripture	12
How to Study the Bible	8	Metanarrative of Scripture	14
The Attributes of God	10	Introduction	16

WEEK 1: GOSPEL HOPE FOR THE HARD DAYS OF MOTHERHOOD — 18

Week 1 Introduction & Memory Verse	20	Day 4: Jesus Is Strong When We Are Weak	45
Day 1: The Gospel and Motherhood	23	Day 5: Gospel Hope for Weary Moms	53
Extra: Prayer Prompts for Moms	28	Day 5: End-of-Week Reflection	56
Day 2: Ideals vs. Reality	31	Days 6–7: Week 1 Application	58
Day 3: A Biblical Vision for Motherhood	37		

WEEK 2: BIBLICAL HOPE FOR OUR DIFFICULT EMOTIONS PART 1 — 61

Week 2 Introduction & Memory Verse	62	Day 4: Despair	85
Day 1: Guilt	65	Day 5: Loneliness	91
Day 2: Anger	71	Day 5: End-of-Week Reflection	96
Day 3: Anxiety	77	Days 6–7: Week 2 Application	98
Extra: Prioritizing God's Word as a Busy Mom	82		

WEEK 3: BIBLICAL HOPE FOR OUR DIFFICULT EMOTIONS PART 2   101

Week 3 Introduction & Memory Verse	102	Extra: Teaching Your Children About God	124
Day 1: Discontentment	105	Day 4: Failure	127
Extra: Hymn: "It Is Well with My Soul"	111	Day 5: Control	133
Day 2: Impatience	113	Day 5: End-of-Week Reflection	138
Day 3: Self-Pity	119	Days 6–7: Week 3 Application	140

WEEK 4: BIBLICAL HOPE FOR OUR DIFFICULT EMOTIONS PART 3   143

Week 4 Introduction & Memory Verse	144	Day 4: Laziness	167
Day 1: Exhaustion	147	Day 5: Overwhelm	173
Day 2: Comparison	153	Day 5: End-of-Week Reflection	178
Day 3: Dissatisfaction	159	Days 6–7: Week 4 Application	180
Extra: Brainstorm: Ways to Connect with Your Children	164		

WEEK 5: GOD'S GRACE IS SUFFICIENT FOR MOTHERHOOD   183

Week 5 Introduction & Memory Verse	184	Day 4: Jesus Is with Us in the Trenches	207
Day 1: Count the Days (They Are Limited)	187	Day 5: Labor Pains: He Is Coming Again	213
Day 2: The Important Work of Mothering (Your Work Matters)	193	Day 5: End-of-Week Reflection	218
Day 3: In Every Daily Stress, His Grace is Sufficient	199	Days 6–7: Week 5 Application	220

Study Suggestions

We believe that the Bible is true, trustworthy, and timeless and that it is vitally important for all believers. These study suggestions are intended to help you more effectively study Scripture as you seek to know and love God through His Word.

SUGGESTED STUDY TOOLS

- ☐ Bible

- ☐ Double-spaced, printed copy of the Scripture passages that this study covers (You can use a website like www.biblegateway.com to copy the text of a passage and print out a double-spaced copy to be able to mark on easily.)

- ☐ Journal to write notes or prayers

- ☐ Pens, colored pencils, and highlighters

- ☐ Dictionary to look up unfamiliar words

Pray

Begin your study time in prayer. Ask God to reveal Himself to you, help you understand what you are reading, and transform you with His Word (Psalm 119:18).

 ## Read Scripture

Before you read what is written in each day of the study itself, read the assigned passages of Scripture for that day. Use your double-spaced copy to circle, underline, highlight, draw arrows, and mark in any way you would like to help you dig deeper as you work through a passage.

 ## Memorize Scripture

Each week of the study begins with a memory verse. You may want to write the verse down and put it in a place where you will see it often. We also recommend spending a few minutes memorizing the verse before you complete each day's study material.

 ## Read Study Content

Read the daily written content provided for the current study day.

 ## Respond

Answer the questions that appear at the end of each study day.

How to Study the Bible

The inductive method provides tools for deeper and more intentional Bible study. To study the Bible inductively, work through the steps below after reading background information on the book.

Observation & Comprehension
KEY QUESTION: WHAT DOES THE TEXT SAY?

After reading the daily Scripture in its entirety at least once, begin working with smaller portions of the Scripture. Read a passage of Scripture repetitively, and then mark the following items in the text:

- Key or repeated words and ideas
- Key themes
- Transition words (e.g., therefore, but, because, if/then, likewise, etc.)
- Lists
- Comparisons and contrasts
- Commands
- Unfamiliar words (look these up in a dictionary)
- Questions you have about the text

Interpretation
KEY QUESTION: WHAT DOES THE TEXT MEAN?

Once you have annotated the text, work through the following steps to help you interpret its meaning:

- Read the passage in other versions for a better understanding of the text.
- Read cross-references to help interpret Scripture with Scripture.
- Paraphrase or summarize the passage to check for understanding.
- Identify how the text reflects the metanarrative of Scripture, which is the story of creation, fall, redemption, and restoration.
- Read trustworthy commentaries if you need further insight into the meaning of the passage.

Application

Bible study is not merely an intellectual pursuit. The truths about God, ourselves, and the gospel that we discover in Scripture should produce transformation in our hearts and lives. Answer the following questions and prompts as you consider what you have learned in your study:

- What attributes of God's character are revealed in the passage?

- Consider places where the text directly states the character of God, as well as how His character is revealed through His words and actions.

- What do I learn about myself in light of who God is?

- Consider how you fall short of God's character, how the text reveals your sin nature, and what it says about your new identity in Christ.

- How should this truth change me?

- A passage of Scripture may contain direct commands telling us what to do or warnings about sins to avoid in order to help us grow in holiness. Other times, our application flows out of seeing ourselves in light of God's character. As we pray and reflect on how God is calling us to change in light of His Word, we should be asking questions like, "How should I pray for God to change my heart?" and "What practical steps can I take toward cultivating habits of holiness?"

The Attributes of God

Eternal

God has no beginning and no end. He always was, always is, and always will be.

HAB. 1:12 / REV. 1:8 / ISA. 41:4

Faithful

God is incapable of anything but fidelity. He is loyally devoted to His plan and purpose.

2 TIM. 2:13 / DEUT. 7:9 / HEB. 10:23

Good

God is pure; there is no defilement in Him. He is unable to sin, and all He does is good.

GEN. 1:31 / PS. 34:8 / PS. 107:1

Gracious

God is kind, giving us gifts and benefits we do not deserve.

2 KINGS 13:23 / PS. 145:8 ISA. 30:18

Holy

God is undefiled and unable to be in the presence of defilement. He is sacred and set-apart.

REV. 4:8 / LEV. 19:2 / HAB. 1:13

Incomprehensible

God is high above and beyond human understanding. He is unable to be fully known.

PS. 145:3 / ISA. 55:8-9 ROM. 11:33-36

Immutable

God does not change. He is the same yesterday, today, and tomorrow.

1 SAM. 15:29 / ROM. 11:29 JAMES 1:17

Infinite

God is limitless. He exhibits all of His attributes perfectly and boundlessly.

ROM. 11:33-36 / ISA. 40:28 PS. 147:5

Jealous

God is desirous of receiving the praise and affection He rightly deserves.

EXOD. 20:5 / DEUT. 4:23-24 JOSH. 24:19

Just

God governs in perfect justice. He acts in accordance with justice. In Him, there is no wrongdoing or dishonesty.

ISA. 61:8 / DEUT. 32:4 / PS. 146:7-9

Loving

God is eternally, enduringly, steadfastly loving and affectionate. He does not forsake or betray His covenant love.

JOHN 3:16 / EPH. 2:4-5 / 1 JOHN 4:16

Merciful

God is compassionate, withholding from us the wrath that we deserve.

TITUS 3:5 / PS. 25:10 LAM. 3:22-23

Omnipotent

God is all-powerful;
His strength is unlimited.

MATT. 19:26 / JOB 42:1-2
JER. 32:27

Omnipresent

God is everywhere;
His presence is near
and permeating.

PROV. 15:3 / PS. 139:7-10
JER. 23:23-24

Omniscient

God is all-knowing;
there is nothing
unknown to Him.

PS. 147:4 / I JOHN 3:20
HEB. 4:13

Patient

God is long-suffering and
enduring. He gives ample
opportunity for people
to turn toward Him.

ROM. 2:4 / 2 PET. 3:9 / PS. 86:15

Self-Existent

God was not created
but exists by His
power alone.

PS. 90:1-2 / JOHN 1:4 / JOHN 5:26

Self-Sufficient

God has no needs
and depends on
nothing, but everything
depends on God.

ISA. 40:28-31 / ACTS 17:24-25
PHIL. 4:19

Sovereign

God governs over
all things; He is in
complete control.

COL. 1:17 / PS. 24:1-2
1 CHRON. 29:11-12

Truthful

God is our measurement
of what is fact. By Him
we are able to discern
true and false.

JOHN 3:33 / ROM. 1:25 / JOHN 14:6

Wise

God is infinitely
knowledgeable and
is judicious with
His knowledge.

ISA. 46:9-10 / ISA. 55:9 / PROV. 3:19

Wrathful

God stands in opposition
to all that is evil. He enacts
judgment according to
His holiness, righteousness,
and justice.

PS. 69:24 / JOHN 3:36 / ROM. 1:18

Timeline of Scripture

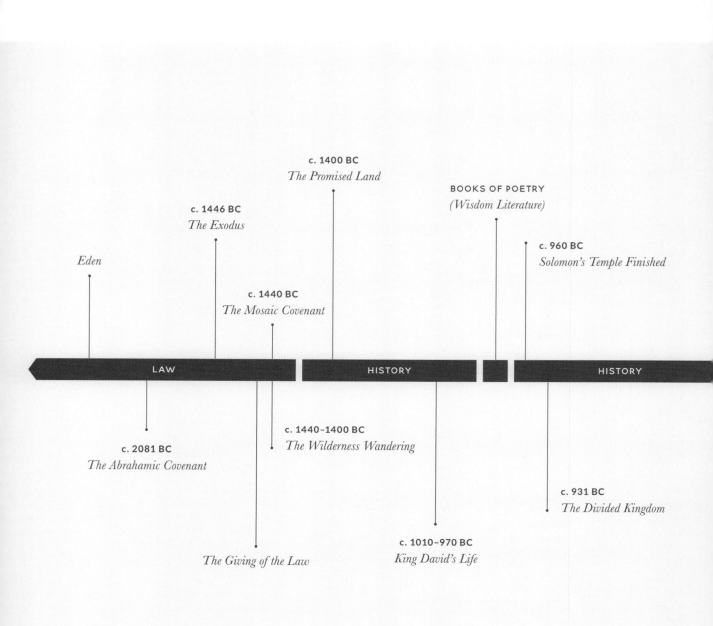

c. 1400 BC
The Promised Land

BOOKS OF POETRY
(Wisdom Literature)

c. 1446 BC
The Exodus

c. 960 BC
Solomon's Temple Finished

Eden

c. 1440 BC
The Mosaic Covenant

LAW   HISTORY   HISTORY

c. 2081 BC
The Abrahamic Covenant

c. 1440–1400 BC
The Wilderness Wandering

c. 931 BC
The Divided Kingdom

The Giving of the Law

c. 1010–970 BC
King David's Life

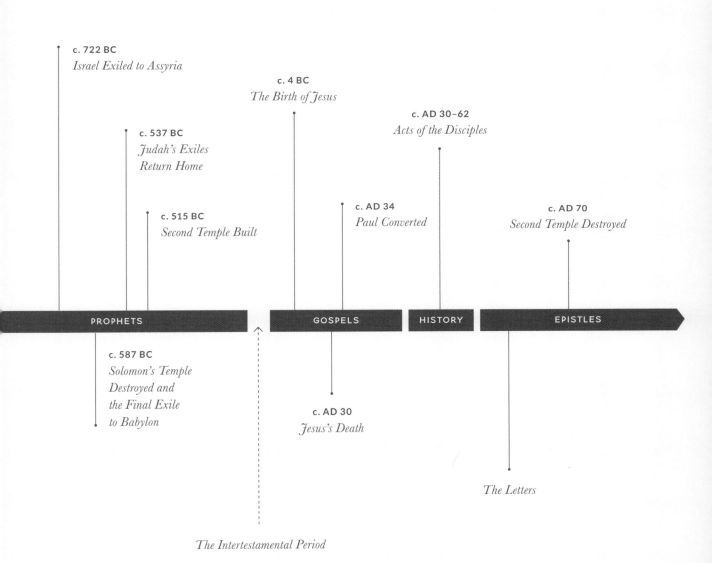

c. 722 BC
Israel Exiled to Assyria

c. 4 BC
The Birth of Jesus

c. AD 30–62
Acts of the Disciples

c. 537 BC
*Judah's Exiles
Return Home*

c. AD 34
Paul Converted

c. AD 70
Second Temple Destroyed

c. 515 BC
Second Temple Built

PROPHETS

GOSPELS

HISTORY

EPISTLES

c. 587 BC
*Solomon's Temple
Destroyed and
the Final Exile
to Babylon*

c. AD 30
Jesus's Death

The Letters

The Intertestamental Period

Metanarrative
of Scripture

Creation

In the beginning, God created the universe. He made the world and everything in it. He created humans in His own image to be His representatives on the earth.

Fall

The first humans, Adam and Eve, disobeyed God by eating from the fruit of the Tree of Knowledge of Good and Evil. Their disobedience impacted the whole world. The punishment for sin is death, and because of Adam's original sin, all humans are sinful and condemned to death.

Redemption

God sent His Son to become a human and redeem His people. Jesus Christ lived a sinless life but died on the cross to pay the penalty for sin. He resurrected from the dead and ascended into heaven. All who put their faith in Jesus are saved from death and freely receive the gift of eternal life.

Restoration

One day, Jesus Christ will return again and restore all that sin destroyed. He will usher in a new heaven and new earth where all who trust in Him will live eternally with glorified bodies in the presence of God.

Introduction

Motherhood does not come with a manual, though many of us wish it did.

We learn as we go, quickly discovering that being a mom is simultaneously one of the most beautiful and the most challenging experiences we have ever known. One minute, we are overflowing with love for our children. We are patient, kind, and caring for our kids with model gentleness. The next moment, we are on a wild rampage about who knows what—maybe a dirty room, a child's rebellious attitude, or a bad grade from school. The emotional ups and downs of motherhood can feel confusing and disorienting.

Not only this, but our motherhood journeys are ever-evolving. Just as we "figure out" one stage of motherhood, our children grow and change. We face new joys and challenges as the parental strategies we once relied upon no longer apply.

But while motherhood does not come with a manual, we are not alone. God is with us, and He has given us His perfect, unchanging Word as our guide. The Lord promises to help us in even the most mundane and difficult moments of mothering. He guides us and holds our hand, whether we are nursing newborns or sending freshly graduated high schoolers off to college. He is our refuge and strength always, even through the hardest days of motherhood.

Throughout this five-week study, we will be discussing many of the difficult emotions we can experience as moms, ranging from anger to anxiety. As we dive in, it is our hope that you will find comfort in two truths. First, you are not alone. Experiencing the turbulent roller coaster of emotions is a normal part of motherhood. Second, there is hope for every difficult emotion in Christ. He cares about what we feel, and He offers us hope for every challenging moment.

As you complete this study, you will notice that each week begins with a memory verse. It may be helpful to write each verse down and place it somewhere you will see it often. We recommend spending a few moments each day reviewing your verses before you complete the study material in order to renew your mind in the truths of God's Word. You can also practice your memory verses while making snacks for your toddler, sitting in the carpool line, or rocking your baby in the middle of the night.

Finally, as you work through this study, know that we are praying for you. We are praying that God gives you renewed hope and comfort in Christ throughout every moment of your mothering. Though we may struggle with our emotions in motherhood, God is with us. There is no part of your mothering that is beyond God's reach. He helps us and cares for us each and every second.

May the Lord strengthen your faith, hope, love, and endurance through this study as you aim to love Him and your children well.

"There is no part of your mothering that is beyond God's reach."

"I always wanted to be a hero — to sacrifice my life in a big way one time — and yet, God has required my sacrifice to be thousands of days, over many years, with one more kiss, one more story, one more meal."

Sally Clarkson

(2013)

Gospel Hope for the Hard Days of Motherhood

Week 1 Introduction

As moms, we have been given the great privilege of shepherding little hearts. God has gifted us the sacred responsibility of loving, teaching, and caring for our children—little souls who are created in the image of God. But even though motherhood is an incredible gift, it is not always easy. As moms, we are regularly pushed beyond our limits. Our patience is tested, and our emotions are pulled in every possible direction. But thankfully, God is with us on this journey of motherhood. He is our ever-present friend, always leading us and helping us by His perfect love.

Over the next week, we will be setting the foundation for this study by talking about how the gospel changes everything, including how we view our difficult days of motherhood. We will specifically focus on the following truths:

Our greatest joy and hope is found in Christ alone, not in perfectly clean houses or kind and rational toddlers.	God has given us a great purpose as moms to love, lead, and teach our children about the Lord.	Even on our hard days, God is always with us. He is strong when we are weak.

As you prepare for this study week, pray that the Lord would give you a hunger for His Word and that He would draw you nearer to Himself. Reflect also on the following questions:

How has your motherhood journey been different from what you expected?	How have you experienced the hope of Christ on your difficult days of mothering?	What would it look like for you to have confidence in God's love for you, even on the hard days?

MEMORY VERSE

2 Corinthians 12:9

But he said to me, "My grace is
sufficient for you, for my power is
perfected in weakness." Therefore,
I will most gladly boast all the more
about my weaknesses, so that
Christ's power may reside in me.

THE GOSPEL CHANGES
EVERYTHING. IT BRINGS US
HOPE FOR TOMORROW AND
STRENGTH FOR TODAY.

Day 1

Ephesians 1:4-6
1 Corinthians 15:1-6
1 John 3:1

—

Practice this week's
memory verse
on page 21.

The Gospel and Motherhood

Newborn cries fill the anticipative hospital room. You have never heard anything so beautiful in your life. Your exhaustion immediately vanishes as you relish the sounds of your new baby, and with each passing second, you breathe a deeper sigh of relief. You did it. Your baby is here, and she is beautiful. Within moments, her pink little fingers wrap around yours, the thrilling intertwining of life on life. As you lay your baby on your chest, counting every finger and kissing every toe, you thank God for this exquisite gift of new life.

Or perhaps, your birth story was not quite so picturesque. Your birth plans were hastily thrown out the window as unforeseen complications, miscommunications, and health scares led to a difficult delivery. A long road of recovery lay ahead, ushering along with it anxiety and worry about the well-being of your child. Or maybe you became a mother through the long and emotional process of adoption. It was not easy, but after years of painful waiting, the beautiful child in your arms makes it all worth it.

Regardless of your birth story, age, or season of life, if you are a mom, you know: motherhood is a gift. It is an incredible blessing from God to be called "mom." Yet at the same time, it can also be a difficult calling, full of countless ups and downs. One moment, you cannot believe that you have been blessed with the smartest, most incredible, most gifted child in the world. The next moment, you are brought rudely back to reality as your son takes a jet-black Sharpie to your freshly painted walls or as your daughter jams a wad of stringy, sticky bubble gum deep into her beautiful bouncing curls. Your emotions within motherhood can change faster than the unpredictable tenor of a toddler's temper tantrum.

Thankfully, there is hope for us—even through the difficult emotions of motherhood—because of the gospel of Jesus Christ. The gospel shows us not only how to be saved but also how to live godly lives. It provides hope and purpose to every season, including our seasons of motherhood.

The message of the gospel is this: Jesus came to save us from our sins by dying for us on the cross and rising again from the grave. Through His death, we are forgiven, and through His life, we are given new hope and everlasting life.

As moms, young or old, our hope is secure in Jesus. The reality is that we all had an eternal problem that we could not fix. Though we tried to make ourselves good enough on our own, our sins separated us from God. Even seemingly "minor" sins, such as impatience, anger, envy, and faithlessness, captured and condemned us. Our hearts and our hands were dirty. But thankfully, God had a plan to rescue us from our hopeless state by sending His Son, Jesus, to save us (1 Corinthians 15:1–6).

Often we want to be "good enough" moms for our children, yet embarrassingly, we fall short every single day. But when Jesus came to earth, He lived a perfect life. He was never impatient. He never rashly lost His temper, tearing others down in a fit of unjust rage. He flawlessly loved those around Him and was perfectly patient, loving, and kind. Not only this, but Jesus sacrificed Himself and took the punishment that we deserved, dying on the cross for our sins and washing us clean (1 John 1:9). Through His life, death, and resurrection, Jesus destroyed the power of sin and death in our lives, setting us free from our bondage to sin. Now, after we believe in Jesus, He gives us His Spirit to live inside of us to guide us and help us each day.

Because of the gospel, we are no longer slaves to our sin. Instead, we are set free to live in a way that honors Christ. In light of this, our role within parenthood becomes an incredible privilege to point to something even greater than itself: the love of the Father toward us (1 John 3:1). Our heavenly Father is the perfect Parent who chose us before the creation of the world to be His children (Ephesians 1:4–6). In love, God saved us, adopted us, and made us His own. Though we were sinners, rebellious and undeserving of grace, God chose us to become His loved children. God does not love us because we are good enough. He loves us because He is love.

And God's love is not like our own—a fickle, unpredictable, and easily provoked love. His love is better than we could ever imagine. It is unconditional, undeserved, and never-ending. His love changes us, restores us, fills us, and gives us the security to live radically for Him. God's love also helps us in our desire to be "good moms." Because of the gospel, we do not need to muster up enough goodwill or have enough "me time" to love our children well. We can love our children out of the overflow of God's love for us. We love others because God has loved us (1 John 4:19).

If this language feels confusing, and you are wondering how the gospel specifically impacts your hard moments of mothering, you are in the right place. This study will focus on how the gospel provides hope for the difficult emotions we experience within motherhood. But for now, cling to this main point: the gospel changes everything. It brings us hope for tomorrow and strength for today. As moms, we no longer parent on our own. We are not helpless against the pull of difficult emotions, as we will describe further throughout this study. Instead, the Creator of the universe is with us as we parent, and He will help us. He has already solved our greatest problem—eternal condemnation before a holy God—and provided a way for us to be forgiven of our sins. He will not abandon us now. God has set us free and given us new hope through the gospel. There is hope for us in our mothering.

Indeed, the best is yet to come.

"There is hope for us — even through the difficult emotions of motherhood — because of the gospel of Jesus Christ."

Day 1 Questions

How would you like to grow in your understanding of God, motherhood, or emotions through this study?

Read Ephesians 1:4-6. How has your life changed because of the gospel?

Write a prayer to the Lord. Ask God to bless your time in this study, growing your love for and knowledge of Him.

Today's Notes

ATTRIBUTE OF GOD I AM MEDITATING ON TODAY:

REMEMBER THIS:

Prayer Prompts for Moms

PRAYER PROMPTS FOR THE NEXT FIVE WEEKS

Over the next few weeks, we will be discussing several of the negative emotions that can accompany our mothering. As you prepare for this study, pray that the Lord would use this resource to strengthen your faith.

Place this list in a place where you will see it, and pray through it regularly. At the end of this study, revisit this page to see how God has answered your prayers:

- Pray that the Lord will use this study to grow your love for God and His Word. Pray that your affection for Christ will grow and that you will be transformed in His image.

- Pray that God will help you to identify your negative emotions in your mothering and renew your mind according to biblical hope.

- Pray that Jesus will be your greatest hope on the difficult days of mothering. Pray that He will be your greatest treasure, hope, and friend.

- Pray for godly friends who will encourage you in your faith and in your mothering. Pray that you will be an encouragement to them as well.

- Pray that you will grow in love, patience, and joy in your role as a mom.

- Pray for your children—that they will draw closer to the Lord as you seek Him.

CREATE YOUR OWN
PRAYER PROMPTS

GOD'S WORD GIVES
US HOPE FOR OUR
STRUGGLES AND ANSWERS
TO OUR QUESTIONS.

Day 2

Genesis 3:16
Galatians 5:13-18
Ephesians 6:10-20

—

Practice this week's memory verse on page 21.

Ideals vs. Reality

When we become moms, our worlds instantly change. Our priorities shift. Our bodies transform. Our hearts burst with joy as love pushes the bounds of our imaginations and redefines how we understand the word "love." Emotions and experiences we only dreamed about now burst into our lives with vibrant colors. We are simultaneously awed by the beauty of life and humbled by the important responsibility of motherhood. Truly, meeting our children for the first time, whether by birth or by adoption, introduces a beautiful spectrum of human emotions.

But unfortunately, when we become moms, we do not only experience joyful emotions. With love, joy, and humility can come a number of complex emotions such as anxiety, loneliness, and despair. We worry. From the time our children are in the womb, we anxiously wonder, *What's going to happen to my children throughout their lives? What kind of world will they grow up in? How can I protect them from those who want to harm them?* As our children grow, our complex emotions often grow too. Though we may be surrounded by little humans every waking hour, we have never felt so lonely in our lives. We may even despair in motherhood at times, wondering, *Why is this all so hard?*

Thankfully, God's Word gives us hope for our struggles and answers to our questions. After all, the quest for meaning in motherhood did not begin in the twenty-first century. It is a pursuit that started all the way back in the book of Genesis (Genesis 3:16, 29:28–35). Therefore, as we broach the topic of difficult emotions in motherhood, we begin by looking back to the garden of Eden.

In the beginning, when God made the world, He made it good (Genesis 1:31). There was no pain, despair, or confusion. There was no toddler rebellion, teenage acne, or tired and baggy eyes. There was only wholeness and beauty—life and peace. But although God made the world good, He also gave humans the choice to either follow Him or follow the passions of their hearts. The former choice leads to everlasting life and peace; the latter, to momentary pleasure followed by sin and death.

As we see in Genesis 3, Adam and Eve chose the latter and rebelled against God. When Eve was tempted, she questioned God's care for her and wondered if He was withholding something good. When Adam and Eve fell into sin, brokenness was introduced into the world. Now, instead of dwelling in perfect peace with God in the garden, we experience the devastation of sin because of the Fall. Death, pain, sorrow, boo-boos, and fighting become unwanted household guests throughout our mothering years. We experience not only physical pain in childbirth but also relational, spiritual, and emotional pain throughout our entire lives (Genesis 3:16).

Therefore, even as we seek to address some of the difficult emotions in motherhood throughout this study, we are not surprised at their presence. Because of the Fall, we all struggle in various ways. We battle within our homes and within our minds. We strive for peace but face continual conflict. We wrestle against despair and darkness. Ultimately, we know that our true enemy in life is not spilled milk or messy houses. As Paul says, "Our struggle is not against flesh and blood, but against the rulers, against the authorities, against the cosmic powers of this darkness, against evil, spiritual forces in the heavens" (Ephesians 6:12).

Motherhood is an important calling with spiritual significance. God designed our homes to be safe places where our children are loved, honored, and discipled. It is the place where the next generation is to learn about the grace and truth of God. It is no wonder, then, that the home is also the place of real spiritual struggle. But although the effects of sin are very real in our lives, the grace and power of Christ is even greater.

Embedded within the curse found in Genesis 3 is also an important promise: Christ will come again to make all things right (Genesis 3:15). Not only did Jesus die on the cross to set us free from the power of sin and death, but He also rose from the dead to give us new life. He is Adam's ultimate offspring, the Son of God who crushed the head of the enemy, destroying the power of sin in our lives. And one day, He will return again to reign as King forever. There will be no more sin, sadness, or conflict. He will reign forever, and there will be peace.

Therefore, because Jesus saved us, we are not powerless on the difficult days of motherhood. Instead, we can put on the full armor of God by the power of the gospel (Ephesians 6:10–20). We can fix our eyes not on sticky fingers, tiny crumbs, or unending piles of laundry but on the Savior and Lover of our souls. We can fight the good fight of faith in our families, even when our idealistic dreams of motherhood are long forgotten, replaced by years of disappointed realities. We can pursue holiness, not trying to earn God's love but in response to it. We can pray at all times and meditate on the Word of God (Ephesians 6:17–18), believing that He is better than anything the world has to offer. For we place our hope not in what is seen but on what is unseen (2 Corinthians 4:18). Though this world is broken, Jesus is coming again, and He will sustain us until the end.

As we look to Jesus, we remember that He cares for us, and He is coming again. He cares about our difficult emotions, ingrained habits, and tired bodies. He cares about all the little details of our lives because He loves us. He is our compassionate friend, and He is the victorious One. He will restore all things. So when your dreams of motherhood do not match up with your current life, do not despair. Instead, look to Jesus. Though this world is broken, Jesus is good. He is your rest, and He is coming to make all things new (Revelation 21:5).

"Because Jesus saved us, we are not powerless on the difficult days of motherhood. Instead, we can put on the full armor of God by the power of the gospel. We can fix our eyes not on sticky fingers, tiny crumbs, or unending piles of laundry but on the Savior and Lover of our souls."

Day 2 Questions

What ideals or visions did you have for motherhood before you became a mom?

How has your reality been different from your expectations? How do today's verses bring clarity to these differences between ideals and realities?

Read Galatians 5:13–18. How should the freedom of Christ impact your daily life as a mom?

Today's Notes

ATTRIBUTE OF GOD I AM MEDITATING ON TODAY:

REMEMBER THIS:

WE MUST BE DEPENDENT
ON THE LORD FOR ALL
THINGS, INCLUDING LOVING
OUR CHILDREN WELL.

Day 3

Psalm 127
Proverbs 22:6

—

Practice this week's
memory verse
on page 21.

A Biblical Vision for Motherhood

What is the goal of your motherhood? What kind of mom do you want to be, and what are your hopes and dreams for your children? Often as moms, we let culture define the answers to these questions. We long for healthy, happy children who are materially comfortable and socially adept. We strive for accomplished children who get good grades and are avid athletes, flourishing musicians, and generally well-rounded. And while none of these desires for our children are inherently wrong, we tend to look more to modern culture for a vision of motherhood than we look to God.

Even so, the cultural advice around us can be confusing. We can feel overwhelmed as different camps around us loudly compete for our attention, with a wide range of conflicting opinions on the spectrum of breastfeeding or bottle-feeding, co-sleeping or crib sleeping, working outside the home or staying at home. Each parenting philosophy promises us the enviable badge of "good parent," yet we feel lost in our desire to please God and raise godly children. In a swirling sea of contrasting voices, we struggle to find purpose in our mothering.

Praise God that His desire and vision for our motherhood are clear through the Bible. God has not left us alone to figure out how to be faithful mothers. He has not abandoned us to navigate the confusing cultural trends on our own. Instead, He has given us everything that we need for life and godliness through His Word.

So what is a biblical vision of motherhood? In the Bible, God gives us the honor and privilege of becoming a mom for several purposes, including the call to love, nurture, and instruct our children in the faith. Let's dive deeper into each calling:

Love

Our primary role as parents is not to make prodigy pianists or budding engineers but to point our children toward the love of God. In motherhood, we have the unique privilege of loving our children. Indeed, God has given moms the unique and important responsibility of being a picture of the Father's love for us (Isaiah 49:15). Within this calling, we are called to love our children at all times—when they are cute, clean, and surprisingly obedient *and* when they are testing the bounds of our patience with grumpy attitudes. But how do we love our children when they are stinky, moody, or melting down in the middle of the grocery store? How do we love our toddler well when our blood is boiling because he just destroyed our antique vase in a burst of mischievous energy? Or how do we love the rebellious teenager who is sneaking out of the house and pushing every carefully communicated boundary? As today's psalm teaches us, we must be dependent on the Lord for all things, including loving our children well. We love because God loved us.

In Psalm 127, Solomon wrote about dependence on the Lord (Akin and Smith, 2021, 215). His words remind us that we do not parent out of our own strength but with complete dependence on the Lord. Without God, we labor in vain. We count to three, take deep breaths, and bark out orders in frustration. We read parenting books and ask other moms for advice. We get up early and stay up late, yielding no fruit for our labors. Without God's grace, even our best-made plans are fruitless.

But with God, there is rest, hope, and peace. As we remember God's steadfast love and prayerfully depend on Him, God helps, equips, and changes us. As we depend on God, we remember His love for us—a love that is not dependent on our good deeds. We have the opportunity to point our children toward the love and grace of God, even when they do not deserve it. And

even when we fail in the weighty calling of loving our children well, we can use our failures as another opportunity to remind our children: though we fail, there is One who never does.

Children are a blessing (Psalm 127:3–5), and God has given us children for us to love them. It is a great privilege to love our children as Christ has loved us, pointing them toward the unending love of their heavenly Father.

Nurture

Another way that we can love our children is by nurturing them. We care for our children, brushing little teeth and giving nighttime baths. We bandage little boo-boos and tend to wounded hearts. We nurture and care for our children in both tangible and intangible ways.

Just as God cares for our needs and takes care of us (Matthew 6:26), we also take care of our children. We listen to their problems and bless them with good gifts (Luke 11:13). We show our children that motherhood is not a burden; it is a blessing. We show them with our words and with our lives that our children are not inconveniences. They are gifts, beautifully and wonderfully made (Psalm 139:14).

Instruct

A third purpose of motherhood is to instruct our children in the Lord (Deuteronomy 4:9). We teach our children about the One who made them and who loves them. We teach our children about wisdom, integrity, and how to live godly lives. We train our children in the ways that they should go (Proverbs 22:6). Like arrows in the hands of a warrior, we raise up our children to be beacons of truth and light in a dark world (Psalm 127:4). As we instruct our children, we also make disciples, teaching them how to obey God (Matthew 28:18–20) and instructing our children both in the words we speak and in the examples we set.

It is important to note that this list is not exhaustive. God has given us our children as gifts to protect, serve, discipline, and cherish.

Yet through it all, the main goal of our motherhood is not to raise rich, successful children but to be faithful to the Lord. As we love, nurture, and instruct our children, we point them toward the One who loves them, knows them, and created them for His glory.

"It is a great privilege to love our children as Christ has loved us, pointing them toward the unending love of their heavenly Father."

Day 3 Questions

What are the main purposes of your parenting? If a stranger were to evaluate your family calendar or financial spending, what priorities would they say matter most to your family?

Read Matthew 28:18-20. How do these verses apply to your role as a mother?

Of the three characteristics mentioned in today's study day, which do you struggle with the most? Write a prayer to the Lord asking for His help to love, nurture, and instruct your child in the Lord.

Today's Notes

ATTRIBUTE OF GOD I AM MEDITATING ON TODAY:

REMEMBER THIS:

1 Samuel 1:27-28

"I PRAYED FOR THIS BOY,

AND SINCE THE LORD GAVE ME

WHAT I ASKED HIM FOR,

I NOW GIVE THE BOY TO THE LORD.

FOR AS LONG AS HE LIVES,

HE IS GIVEN TO THE LORD."

THEN HE WORSHIPED THE LORD THERE.

OUR GOAL IS NOT
TO BE PERFECT MOMS
BUT SIMPLY TO POINT TO
THE PERFECT SAVIOR.

Day 4

2 Corinthians 4

—

Practice this week's
memory verse
on page 21.

Jesus Is Strong When We Are Weak

You have the best of intentions to wake up early. Your alarm is set with enough time to exercise, drink coffee, and read God's Word before the baby wakes up. But somehow, your baby always knows. With seemingly telepathic powers, she wakes up right before your alarm, no matter how many changes you make to the clock. Topped off with frequent night feedings, you are so tired that your brain feels vacant. If you blink too often, you are afraid you will fall asleep standing up.

Or maybe, your children are older. In their teenage years, your kids will sleep until the afternoon if you let them. But though you are not as physically exhausted as in the newborn days, you are emotionally worn. Stress has compounded in your life for years, building up to an insurmountable height. College applications, teenage hormones, and fear of the future color your days. You are tired, heavy, and weak.

For tired and weary moms of all stages, there is good news in the gospel: Though we are weak, Christ is strong. Though we faint with burdens and troubles, God never does. He never gets stumped about a math problem or is unsure of what to do. He never forgets what He was doing or loses His keys. He always listens, always protects, and always loves. He leads and guides us perfectly. Jesus is our hope and strength in weary days.

In 2 Corinthians 4, Paul speaks openly of his weakness and Christ's strength. He explains that though he is being destroyed (verse 16) and given over to death (verse 11), he does not give up (verse 16). And within this, he provides the secret for enduring suffering well: by looking to Christ (verses 17–18).

We are weak. In 2 Corinthians 4:7–18, Paul explains that we have the treasure of Christ's gospel hidden within us. That means we have the all-powerful message of salvation hidden within our tired bodies. To the weary mom, this can feel ironic. Like jars of clay in the hands of a clumsy toddler, we feel the vulnerability of our condition (verse 7).

Our lives are not easy, and our emotions often reflect this reality. Suffering and stress weigh us down, and we feel afflicted in every way (verse 8). We are asked to persevere through explosive teenage attitudes, financial struggles, relational stress, and uncertain tomorrows. We are anxious and weak—sleep-deprived, over-touched, and over-stressed. We are worn down with difficult emotions and situations yet entrusted with the most important message and purpose of all: the gospel.

When we are weak, Christ is strong (2 Corinthians 12:9). Even when we feel frail and fragile, we can rejoice in the impenetrability and beauty of Christ. We can withstand suffering with patience because we know that God is with us, and He is working something wonderful through our struggles, often in ways we cannot see (2 Corinthians 4:14–15, 17). We can "press in," even through the emotional and physical pain points of motherhood, because Christ is with us. God's plans are perfect, and He knows what He is doing.

Not only is Jesus with us, but He also died for us to make us right with God. Now, in response to His love, we also have the opportunity to die to ourselves daily—both for Jesus's sake (2 Corinthians 4:10–11) and for the sake of others (verse 15). We can love and serve our families in costly ways and with little recognition because Christ sees us, and He supplies all we need.

Though mothering is difficult, He gives us strength to endure. For as Paul says, though we are afflicted, we are not crushed. Though we are struck down, we are not destroyed (verse 9). We identify with the sufferings and death of Jesus in the difficulties of mothering so that Christ may get the glory in our lives (verse 11).

Therefore, as we endure difficulties, we look not to what is seen—whether piles of homework or increasing wrinkles or loads of laundry—but to what is unseen (verse 18). We remember that God is using our suffering to prepare us for an eternal weight of glory (verse 17). He promises to raise us with Christ and bring us into His presence (verse 14) and to use every struggle for our good (Romans 8:28). And through these seasons of faith, God extends grace to our families for His glory (2 Corinthians 4:15).

Often, when we are tired as moms, we can be tempted to look inward. We rely on lingering reserves of "supermom strength" and find hope in the assurances of future self-care. But Scripture calls us not to look inward but upward (verses 16–18). It calls us to look not to ourselves when we are weak but to Christ, who never is. Like Paul, our mission is not to point toward our own strength or sufficiency but to God's. Our goal is not to be perfect moms but simply to point to the perfect Savior.

We can depend on God not just for the "big moments" of mothering but also for every mundane moment in life. When we experience difficult emotions, exhaustion, and suffering, we know our neediness. We are desperate for the Savior. Yet through it all—through the conflict, the stress, and the changing newborn sleep schedules—we look not to our own wisdom but to Christ's. He is strong enough to carry it all.

In light of the gospel, we do not lose heart even when we are tired. For we know that we have this treasure in clay jars. But though we are weak, Christ is strong. He is our stronghold, and He will keep us until the end.

"We can love and serve our families in costly ways and with little recognition because Christ sees us, and He supplies all we need."

Day 4 Questions

How do you typically cope with stress in motherhood?

Read 2 Corinthians 12:9-10. What do you learn about weakness from these verses?

In what ways do you feel weak as a mother? How is Christ strong enough for those specific needs?

Today's Notes

ATTRIBUTE OF GOD I AM MEDITATING ON TODAY:

REMEMBER THIS:

"God never calls you to a task without giving you what you need to do it. He never sends you without going with you."

PAUL TRIPP (2016)

WE CAN CLING TO
GOD'S UNCHANGING
CHARACTER IN THE MIDST
OF THIS STRESS.

Gospel Hope for Weary Moms

You are tired. You are just *so* tired. Anxiety, despair, and discontentment wrestle sneakily, yet aggressively, within your heart. You regularly compare yourself to other moms who seem to have it all together—or who at least did not forget their children's school lunch boxes, again. The other moms around you seem to have a mysterious strength under pressure, able to cook their children organic meals, remain active in the PTA, and have booming careers, all with a baby on their hip. You, on the other hand, have a growing mental list of all the areas you have fallen short for today alone. (And that list, you might add, is looking rather long.) The pressures of motherhood are enough to make anyone feel tired.

We all can grow weary, especially in difficult seasons of life. Motherhood exposes and challenges us in ways we could never have imagined—physically, spiritually, and emotionally. Like David in Psalm 16, our thoughts can trouble us in the night as sleep evades us (verse 7) and emotions condemn us. Yet even in our weariness, God is with us. He does not condemn us for our weaknesses or punish us for our tiredness. Rather, He blesses us with everything we need in Himself. He draws us in and reminds us that He is our joy. We are safe in Him, gently led through both seasons of suffering and blessing, according to His perfect wisdom.

As we read in today's psalm, we can cling to God's unchanging character in the midst of this stress. David knows that God is his greatest good, his perfect counselor, and the source of his joy. God is his portion and cup (verse 5), the One who holds his future securely (verse 9). Notice how David responds in the midst of his challenges. David is a mighty king and warrior, yet he does not find hope in his own competence or look to his past victories for comfort. Instead, he looks to God and finds hope in Him. Similarly, in the midst of weariness, we should not look to our past or current performances as moms, whether strong or weak. Instead, we can cling to the perfect record of Christ.

God is our good. The Lord is good when we feel close to Him and when we are running away from Him. He is good when we are crushing the mothering game and when we feel so disappointed with ourselves.

Regardless of what kind of meal we cook our children for dinner or how often we forget to brush our kid's teeth, God is always kind and always good to us. He does not shoot us condemning or disapproving looks when we fail. Rather, He gathers us into His arms and patiently draws us in as our perfect Father. He forgives us, grows us, lovingly corrects us, and strengthens us. He is our strong refuge (verse 1), our faithful Protector (verse 1), and our loving Counselor (verse 7). He is good.

Not only this, but apart from God, we have no good thing (Psalm 16:2, Psalm 73:25). If we have a "perfect day" (however we would define perfection in our current season of motherhood) but we do not have the Lord, we have nothing. He is our greatest joy, and He is sufficient for everything we need today. Every blessing comes from Him.

God is our Counselor. David also knows that God is his guide, the One who leads him every day of his life (Psalm 16:7–8). Similarly, when we are weary from the weight of caring for little humans or from the decision fatigue of motherhood (should we homeschool or send our kids to public school, nurse or bottle feed, co-sleep or crib sleep?), God leads us. In the night, when the baby will not stop crying and we do not know what to do, He helps us. Though God may not speak with audible instructions about how to change a diaper or which nursing schedule to choose, He gives us everything we need for life and godliness through His Word (Psalm 16:7, 2 Peter 1:3). He speaks to us through the Bible, teaching us about His love, care, and patience for us. His Spirit guides us, and He provides us

with community in the local church for support and counsel.

Even more than this, God is our perfect Counselor, the Shepherd of our souls. He is more reliable than an internet search or a twenty-four-hour nurse hotline. He is our constant guide, full of perfect knowledge and wisdom. We can bless the Lord in all seasons, even through the difficult emotions of motherhood, because He is with us (Psalm 16:7–8).

God is our joy. Finally, David knows that God is His ultimate treasure (verses 9–11), and a life with Him is greater than every earthly blessing. In the same way, we can look to Christ for joy in our days of mothering. Contentment is not a goal to be achieved when we have mastered our disciplining strategies or have conflict-free parenting days. It is found in Jesus and is offered to us freely in every season of our lives. God's paths for us are full of abundant pleasures forevermore (verse 11), and if we truly desire lives of happiness, we can run to God to find everlasting joy. He is our treasure, our hope, and our future. We are happiest not when we have perfect children or are finally empty nesters but when we cling to Christ and find our joy in Him.

In our weariness, it can be tempting to withdraw from God. We think that either He will ask more of us in our tiredness or that He will condemn us for our failures. But Scripture tells us that we can run boldly to God when we are weary because He is our help, our hope, and our portion (verse 5). The Lord is our constant help in weary seasons of motherhood. He is our goodness, counsel, and greatest joy.

Day 5 Questions

Where do you typically go for comfort, joy, and counsel? What would it look like for you to run to the Lord in your weariness?

Read Matthew 11:28-30. How does Jesus view weak and weary Christians? What is His offer to them?

Complete the End-of-Week Reflection on the next page.

End-of-Week Reflection

Think back on all of the Scripture that you read and studied this week
as you answer the questions below.

What did you observe about God and His character?

What did you learn about the condition of mankind and yourself?

How did this week's Scripture point to the gospel?

How do the truths you have learned this week about God, man, and the gospel give you hope, peace, and encouragement?

How should you respond to what you read and learned this week? *Write down one or two specific action steps you can take this week to apply what you learned. Then, write a prayer in response to your study of God's Word.*

Week 1 Application

Before we begin a new week of study, take some time to apply
and share the truths of Scripture you learned this week.
Here are a few ideas of how you could do this:

Meet Up

Schedule a meet-up with a friend to share what you are learning
from God's Word.

Worship

Spend time worshiping God in a way that is meaningful to you, whether that is
taking a walk in nature, painting, drawing, singing, etc.

Pray

Use these prompts to journal or pray through what God is revealing to you
through your study of His Word.

• *Lord, I feel . . .*

• *Lord, You are . . .*

• *Lord, forgive me for . . .*

• *Lord, help me with . . .*

Paraphrase

Paraphrase the Scripture you read this week.

Dig Deeper

Use a study Bible or commentary to help you answer questions that came up as you read this week's Scripture.

Take Action

Take steps to fulfill the action steps you listed on Day 5.

Highlight

Use highlighters to mark the places you see the metanarrative of Scripture in one or more of the passages that you read this week. (See "The Metanarrative of Scripture" on page 15.)

"Jesus taught that providing shelter for the shelterless, food for the hungry, and clothing for the naked are sacred acts. They're also the hallmark activities of mothering. When we do them from the right motive for those in our homes, it's as if we've done them for Christ himself (Matt. 25:31-45)."

Jen Wilkin
(2006)

Biblical Hope for Our Difficult Emotions

Part 1

Week 2 Introduction

This week, we will dive into five of the difficult emotions we can experience in motherhood: guilt, anger, anxiety, despair, and loneliness. As we learn about these emotions, we discover that God has offered us very practical hope in the Bible. God cares for our emotions, and He has provided encouragement and strength through His Word.

Over the next five days, we will meditate primarily on the following ideas:

Jesus cares for us. He provides truth, hope, and grace for our difficult emotions as moms.

Even when we fail, we can joyfully repent, knowing that God is merciful and quick to forgive.

God is our joy, Rock, and closest friend. He does not pull back from us when we experience difficult emotions. Rather, He invites us in.

As you prepare for this week of the study, pray that you will find comfort and delight in Christ alone. Pray that the Lord will convict you of sin and lead you to rest confidently in His abundant grace. Reflect also on the following questions:

What did you learn about God's kindness and compassion for you last week?

Which of the five emotions listed above have you struggled with the most?

How does it encourage you that Christ is always with you as your closest friend?

MEMORY VERSE

Romans 8:1

Therefore, there is
now no condemnation for
those in Christ Jesus.

WHEN WE
FEEL INSUFFICIENT,
WE CAN REST IN
THE SUFFICIENCY
OF CHRIST.

Day 1

Romans 8:1
Psalm 32
—
Practice this week's
memory verse
on page 63.

Guilt

Mom guilt. It is a humbling companion for many moms. It follows us as we take care of our children during the day. It condemns us as we lay our tired heads down at night. And although the detailed captions of our guilt may vary from mom to mom, they always have a common thread: failure.

Maybe your variety of mom guilt looks like one of these:

I can't believe that I forgot my child's soccer uniform today. All the parents must be talking about it. My child is so disappointed in me. I'm so disorganized. And come to think of it, our house is always such a mess. No wonder I can't find anything . . .

My child is falling short in their reading. . . I should have started reading to her earlier. I should have signed her up for tutoring last summer. I should be reading in front of her more often. I'm setting her up to fail . . .

Ugh, I lost it again. I can't believe I lost my temper. What is wrong with me? Why can't I just hold this all together? I'm just not cut out to be a good mom . . .

With mom guilt, our thoughts condemn us because of real or perceived failures. Shame overwhelms us as we realize that we are not perfect. We turn inward and carefully critique all the ways in which we have fallen short as moms.

Typically, our guilt can take on two narratives: "I'm not enough" or "I did something wrong." Because we are fallen, limited people, there can be truth to both statements. Honestly, we are not enough for our children, no matter what our days look like. Even if our lives revolve around our kids and we cater to their every need, we are not enough for them. Our children were made for God, and only He can satisfy the deepest desires of their hearts. If we try to fill the role of "savior" in their lives, not only will we be crushed under the weight of impossible expectations, but we will hinder the need for our children to run to Christ themselves. When we feel insufficient, we can rest in the sufficiency of Christ.

But what about when we have truly sinned against our children? We did not just forget to pick up our child's science fair materials from the store; we yelled at them with the full force of our wrath, and now we feel guilty.

Sometimes, we can feel mom guilt because of actual sins we have committed. We were angry with our children, again. We were thoughtless or impatient, again. We poorly managed our time, again. And afterward, we hold on to our sins, nursing deep shame and regret.

As we see in Psalm 32, when we hold on to our sins and run from the Lord, our strength is sapped (verses 3–4), but when we run to the Lord, we find forgiveness (verses 5–6). This means that if we have sinned against our children in any way, we can run to Christ to receive His abundant grace. We should also go to our children and ask for their forgiveness, modeling hearts of humility, godliness, and repentance. As we repent of our sins before God and before our children, we can rest secure in the finished work of Jesus, who paid for every sin on the cross.

If you are feeling guilty, either because of sins committed or because of normal, human limitations, run to the Lord. Scripture tells us that there is no condemnation for those who are in Christ Jesus (Romans 8:1). He has forgiven us of every sin (Psalm 32:1), and He does not count our sins against us (verse 2). Instead, He covers over our every shame when we place our faith in Christ. Now, because of Jesus's finished work on the cross, when God looks at you, He sees the perfection of Christ. You can pray to Him "immediately" for forgiveness (verse 6), knowing that He does not condemn you. He forgives you, counsels you, helps you, and heals you (verses 8–10).

Though we are not enough, God is, and He is abundantly gracious to us. Though we tend to magnify our failures and forget God's grace in our motherhood, we can remember that in Scripture, God is described as the One who sees (Genesis 16:13). He sees everything—the good and the bad moments of our mothering. He sees the times we mess up, as well as all the times we do well—the moments we love our children, the boo-boos we kiss, the soccer uniforms we do remember, and the lunch boxes we carefully pack. God does not count our insufficiencies to hold them over our heads, reciting them over and over. He sees all and provides grace for all, including every single moment we love our children. He will give us the grace we need to continue to love our children more each day.

Throughout all of our victories and failures, we have the incredible opportunity to point our children to the hope of Jesus. He is the One we all need, and His grace is enough for us. Even in our weaknesses, we can remind our children of the complete sufficiency of Christ. For though we may forget things, God never does. Though we cannot be everywhere all at once (as much as we try), Christ is. We are simply not enough for all the needs of our children, but Jesus always will be.

So when guilt plagues you with the feeling of "I'm not enough," rejoice in the Lord. No, you are not enough, but Christ is.

"Because of Jesus's finished work on the cross, when God looks at you, He sees the perfection of Christ."

Day 1 Questions

Write down the times you have experienced mom guilt in the past week. Honestly evaluate: are these areas of godly conviction of sin or unrealistic expectations? If you are unsure, ask a friend or your spouse to help you determine the source of your mom guilt.

Read Isaiah 1:18 and Micah 7:18-19. What is God's offer for your sins today?

Spend time praying and repenting over any sins from question one. Now, write the word FORGIVEN over your list, remembering God's abundant grace for you even when you fail.

Today's Notes

ATTRIBUTE OF GOD I AM MEDITATING ON TODAY:

REMEMBER THIS:

WE CAN RUN TO THE
LORD WHEN WE ARE
ANGRY AND ASK FOR HIS
FORGIVENESS AND HELP.

Day 2

Proverbs 29:11
Ephesians 4:20-31

—

Practice this week's
memory verse
on page 63.

Anger

You cannot believe you lost it again. Before you had kids, you did not think you were a very angry person, but motherhood seems to have brought it out of you. A single look of disrespect, an unreasonable toddler, or a spilled bowl of cereal is enough to set you off. Now, your anger feels uncontrollable. It regularly bubbles up within you until angry words explode with a vengeance. Maybe you raise your voice, slam the door, or bang your fist on the table as expressions of frustration come tumbling out of your mouth—with words and tones that you would be embarrassed to express in front of any other person.

Although our anger in motherhood can feel isolating and impossible to resist, there is hope. Scripture regularly talks about anger because it is a normal part of the human experience. God actually made the emotion of anger, and anger is a recognition that there are wrongs that happen in the world. God Himself is angered by these wrongs—from major injustices to the daily sins we battle. But His anger is not like our own (James 1:20). God's anger never flies off the handle or loses control. It is perfectly pure, just, and holy.

Our anger, on the other hand, is often sinful and self-centered. Our anger reveals that something we treasure is being threatened, from sleep to "me time." We forget that we have all that we need in Christ, and we get personally offended. We must have what we want, whether that be respect or peace and quiet. And when we do not get what we want, we lash out in anger (Groves 2019).

In the book of Ephesians, Paul speaks to our anger problems directly. Throughout the book, he writes to the church at Ephesus about the beauty and sufficiency of Christ. He explains that being a Christian changes how we live in every way (Ephesians 4:20–23), including how we view our tempers. Because Christ has forgiven us, we are to speak kindly, forgive others, and live holy lives (verse 32). To further explain this point, Paul uses an important analogy: that of "putting off" and "putting on" (verses 20–25). Like a soiled onesie, we are to "put off" the dirty deeds of ungodliness and "put on" clothes of righteousness.

But what does this look like practically in our mothering? To start, Paul says that we are to put off anger and put on self-control. Specifically, Paul calls us to speak the truth in every season (verses 24–25). When we are angry as moms, it can be easy to exaggerate consequences with statements such as, "If you don't calm down, I'm never buying you a toy again!" Or, "Stop complaining or we're never going to the store again!" Our children know these are empty threats, and our dramatic amplification loses its intended effect. Instead, Scripture calls us to speak the truth in love and not to exaggerate our punishments in frustration.

Scripture also encourages us not to sin when we are angry (verse 26). The phrase "be angry and do not sin" assumes that we will be angry in life. In parenting, there will be moments when we are provoked to anger because our children do something wrong. Maybe our children are not behaving correctly, or they are fighting too much. Maybe they are acting immaturely or making bad decisions. Even so, Scripture affirms that when we are angry, we should not sin. We should not let our anger grow out of control through fits of rage, nor should we let it grow into a cold, settled bitterness. Instead, we are to trust in the Lord and forgive as He forgave us (verse 32).

Without question, we have an essential role to play in the discipline of our children, but becoming sinfully angry neither helps our children nor alleviates our problems long-term. Although we may be able to stop our children from fighting with a quick yell, when we do this, we are not equipping them in future conflict resolution. Therefore, instead of quick, ineffective bursts of anger, we should pray for our children and lovingly discipline them for their own good, not simply because they inconvenienced us.

In verse 27, Paul continues with this theme of anger, going so far as to link anger with spiritual warfare. As discussed in week 1, motherhood is full of difficult emotions. However, as Paul argues, we should not give Satan a foothold in our emotions. The word picture Paul uses here is meant to paint the picture of letting the devil into our house or giving him a room (Osborne, 2017). When we lash out in anger or let bitterness grow in our hearts, we give the enemy room to fester division and disunity within our homes. But as Christian moms, we do not want to be like a city without walls, vulnerable to the attack of the enemy (Proverbs 25:28, 29:11). We want to protect our homes and to live self-controlled lives that honor the Lord by speaking what is helpful and giving grace to our children.

So what if you feel convicted about your anger and want to change, but you do not know how? The first step is to admit your need for Jesus. Our children are not to blame for our anger. We alone are responsible for our heart's disposition and attitudes. We are accountable for our own sins, but thankfully, God forgives us of every sin through Christ. He does not leave us where we are. He brings conviction when we rashly "blow off steam" and when we quickly respond to our children with passive-aggressive comments. He can help us change and grow, even in our most ingrained patterns of anger (Romans 6:6). We can run to the Lord when we are angry and ask for His forgiveness and help.

God's unmerited grace allows us to put on the clothing of Christ so that we can build up our families with our words (Ephesians 4:29). We cannot change on our own, but by God's grace, we can search the Scriptures, find godly examples, and seek counsel from other moms to grow in this area. God promises that He will help us (1 Corinthians 10:13). He will help us to treat our children with gentleness, even when they fail. He will help us to discipline in love, patiently correcting with kindness.

And when we mess up—when we are sinfully angry again, despite our best efforts—we can run to the Lord. He is faithful, and His mercies are new every morning.

As God loves us, so now we are to love others (Ephesians 4:32), trusting in God rather than relying on human anger (James 1:19–20). Let us reflect His love to our children today.

Resource for further study:
Uprooting Anger: Biblical Help for a Common Problem by Robert D. Jones

"Instead of quick, ineffective bursts of anger, we should pray for our children and lovingly discipline them for their own good."

Day 2 Questions

Read James 4:1-2. Why do we fight or get angry?

Spend time reflecting on the most recent time you were angry with your children. What instigated your anger? What felt like it was being threatened (your sanity, rest, respect, etc.)?

Spend time before the Lord in prayer and repent of sinful anger. Ask for His help and ask your child for forgiveness for any ungodly anger.

Today's Notes

ATTRIBUTE OF GOD I AM MEDITATING ON TODAY:

REMEMBER THIS:

IN EACH AND EVERY
SITUATION, OUR STRONG
GOD IS HERE, AND
HE CARES FOR US.

Anxiety

A Beginning Note: At times, our feelings of anxiety can become overwhelming, debilitating, and all-consuming. If you believe that you are struggling with clinical anxiety, please seek the help of a qualified biblical counselor, along with your doctor. Together, these professionals can help direct you to the truths of God's Word while attending to your specific physical, spiritual, and emotional needs.

Your mind is racing. Your back and shoulders feel tight. You cannot take a deep breath. You are anxious. Balancing the demands of motherhood, busy schedules, and family expectations feels suffocating. Maybe your season of motherhood has led to a newfound struggle against anxiety, or maybe it has simply magnified a battle you have had for many years.

Sometimes, your anxieties may even grow to overwhelming proportions. Your feelings of fear morph into full-blown panic attacks as your heart races and the world closes in. If you were to try to narrow down the root cause of your anxiousness, it would feel impossible because you are scared of so many things. You are so scared of the future—of what might happen to your children when you are not looking. You are scared of the power of others—ranging from the influence of friends, to the possibility of car accidents, to bullies at school. You are scared of messing up your children with your parenting, and you are even scared of who you will be after years of sacrificing your own desires as a mom.

When we are afraid, we know that life is dangerous. Motherhood regularly and constantly reminds us that we are not in control. For though we may feed our children each day, we do not give them their every breath. Though we may bathe our children, we cannot shelter them from the dirty corruption of the world. We are not God, and bad things happen in this life. But although scary and difficult circumstances can happen in the world, we do not face each day's troubles on our own (Matthew 6:25–34). We know the One who is greater than our fears, and He is with us.

Today's psalm reminds us that while we are not in control, God is. Our Creator protects us and helps us in every season of our lives. He is with us in seasons of family harmony, when all is well and safe in the world, and He is with us when scary times come in the form of unexplained illnesses, injuries, or rebellion. In each and every situation, our strong God is here, and He cares for us.

In today's reading, the psalmist is not naive to the dangers of this world. Instead, throughout the psalm, he alludes to very scary world events. He mentions world disasters, such as the earth giving way and being thrown into the heart of the sea (verses 2–3). He alludes to wars, battles, and enemies (verses 6–11). Even so, the psalmist finds peace and hope in the Lord. So how does he do this?

He begins by remembering who God is. The psalmist says that God is his refuge and strength, a very present help in times of trouble (verse 1). The psalmist's recollection of who God is reminds us that God is our safety. He is strong, and He is our protector. Our God needs no defender because He is the Warrior King who rules the world with His words. He simply spoke, and the world came into existence (Psalm 33:9). He controls all, and He is the perfect, just judge (Psalm 89:14). He is a refuge to us in the midst of danger.

Not only this, but God is with us as our very present help (Psalm 46:1). Regardless of what happens in our days of motherhood, God will never abandon us. No matter what unexpected stresses or disciplining moments come our way, He is never surprised. The One who holds the whole world in His hands—who knows every grain of sand and numbers every hair on our heads, who parts waters and makes bushes burn with indestructible heat—is with us in times of trouble, giving the grace and strength we need in each moment. Therefore, we do not fear (verse 2)—not because bad things can never happen but because our God is our very present help in times of trouble.

Notice how the psalmist specifically says that at the break of dawn, when the battle begins, God is with him (verses 5, 7). The Lord is not only with him in the battle, but the Lord also has the power to make the wars cease (verse 9). Similarly, even through our metaphorical earthquakes in life, through every form of unexpected tragedy or scary moment of mothering, God controls our days. At times, He gives us the strength to endure the battles of motherhood, and at other times, He gives us victories over the battles. Because of this, we can remain firm even through the scary moments of motherhood. We do not need to be toppled by external problems or internal pressures because our powerful Savior is in control, and He is with us (verses 5, 7).

As we remember God's character and presence, we must also be renewing our minds in God's truth. God says that He is our stronghold and that we can be still and know that He is God (verses 10–11). Yet when we are anxious, we tend to forget God altogether. "Stillness" is the last word that would describe us, as our thoughts race and we fretfully meditate on our fears. Furthermore, even though our worst nightmares have not actually happened, we pretend that they have, replaying them over and over again in our minds. We create mental prisons for ourselves, living within imaginations of worst-case scenarios and forgetting our current realities.

As pastor Eric Bancroft once said, when we are anxious, we often live like future atheists, forgetting that God will be with us should our fears come to pass (Bancroft, 2020, 2021). If what we fear were to actually happen, God would give us the grace we need for each moment. But as it stands, the situation has not actually happened. So if we want to fight against anxiety as moms, we must train our minds to think about what is true (Philippians 4:8).

God knows that we are anxious people, and His Word regularly woos us with comforting assurances not to fear. He knows there are many scary things in this world, but He is greater than our fears. So when anxious thoughts come to mind, remember that God is a compassionate Savior. He is with you as your very present help, and you can bring all your anxieties to the Lord in prayer because He cares for you (Philippians 4:6–7). But not only this, you can ask for the Lord's help to think about what is true and for grace to continue on if your fears do come to pass.

The Lord is our good Father who loves us. He is with us in every battle, and He holds our futures securely in His hands.

Resource for further study:
Running Scared: Fear, Worry, and the God of Rest by Edward T. Welch

"*Regardless of what happens in our days of motherhood, God will never abandon us. No matter what unexpected stresses or disciplining moments come our way, He is never surprised.*"

Day 3 Questions

Write a list of your current fears as a mom. Should those fears come to pass, would God be with you to help you?

Read Psalm 23. How does the image of God as your Shepherd bring you peace?

Read Psalm 56:3 and write the verse below. Spend time meditating on it today.

Today's Notes

ATTRIBUTE OF GOD I AM MEDITATING ON TODAY:

REMEMBER THIS:

Prioritizing God's Word as a Busy Mom

DO YOU STRUGGLE TO PRIORITIZE THE
WORD OF GOD IN YOUR DAILY LIFE?

CONSIDER TRYING ONE OF THESE
TIPS FOR BUSY MOMS!

Keep your Bible open on your kitchen counter, and read a verse or two as you are preparing lunch or snacks.

Set your alarm clock to wake you before your children start the day. If they wake up before your alarm, let them join you on your lap as you read the Bible aloud.

Combine prayer with an activity such as cooking. Every time you start to cook, pray for your family.

Keep a sticky note on your mirror to remind you of the truths of God's Word.

Set an alarm on your phone to remind you to take a break, read the Bible, or pray.

Spend the first few minutes of nap time in prayer or in the Word.

Memorize Scripture together with your children!

IN THE MIDST OF GREAT
SORROW AND GRIEF, WE
CAN FIND COMFORT IN THE
CONSTANT LOVE OF GOD.

Day 4

Psalm 42
Romans 15:13
—
Practice this week's
memory verse
on page 63.

Despair

A Beginning Note: If you have been through a prolonged season of depression or are experiencing suicidal thoughts, seek help. Many moms experience seasons of despair or postpartum depression, and a suicide hotline (number 988, if you live in the United States), along with a trusted biblical counselor, can help you find light in your season of darkness.

You do not want to get out of bed. The future feels bleak. The present feels gray. Life and motherhood are hard, and you cannot imagine a future when it will be any easier. Everything feels meaningless and hopeless—either because the daily grind of motherhood has worn you down or because of a larger season of grief or suffering. Your ongoing struggle against the brokenness of this world and against sin only aggravates your feelings of despair.

We can all get discouraged from time to time, but experiencing despair as moms brings additional complications. After all, we are still moms. Even when we are discouraged or feel depressed, we still have children to take care of. Even if we are low energy and do not want to get out of bed, the baby still needs to be fed and the children still need to be sent off to school. Because of this, during seasons of struggle, we can often feel guilty for not investing more in our children, a feeling which is compounded by a dark and growing sense of numbness.

The psalmist of Psalm 42 also knew what it felt like to despair. His words are raw and pleading, a great example of seeking the Lord in the midst of dark seasons. He is overwhelmingly sad, yet his soul pants within him for the Lord, like a deer panting for water (verse 1). He longs to go to God, even in his despondency (verses 2, 5). Throughout the psalm, he pours out his heart to the Lord, pleading for God's grace (verse 4, 9).

When we feel sad, it can be tempting to run from the Lord. We feel like we have no energy to offer God, so we withdraw from Him, expecting that He is disappointed with us. But amazingly, God actually invites us closer, even in our weariness (Matthew 11:28–30). His heart is tender toward the sad, weak, and wounded. He cares for the hurting and broken, and He will not cast you off. He understands your sorrow and despair (Isaiah 53:3–4), and He draws you in, even in your sadness.

Though tears may be our food (Psalm 42:3) and our souls are in turmoil (verse 5), we can run desperately to the Lord. Though God feels far off and we wonder, *Where are you, God?* (verse 3), we know: He is near. He hears every prayer and catches every tear (Psalm 56:8). He listens, protects, and helps—not only in our eternal fight against sin but also during our everyday feelings of sadness and darkness.

Notice how the psalmist talks to himself, even in his sadness (verses 5–8). Though it may require great effort, he spurs on his heart to remember the Lord and find hope in God alone. In the same way, even when we feel like we have no hope, we can talk to ourselves and remind ourselves of the Lord's peace, purpose, and love. But when we talk to ourselves, what should we say?

Looking to Scripture, we find our answer: throughout Scripture, the saints of God regularly remind themselves of the faithfulness of the Lord (verse 8). Therefore, we should do the same and remind ourselves of the Lord's faithfulness. As it says in Lamentations 3:22–23, "Because of the LORD's faithful love we do not perish, for his mercies never end. They are new every morning; great is your faithfulness!" God is eternally faithful to His children, and the truth that God does not leave us or forsake us can bring us great hope in seasons of darkness.

God does not leave us when we do not want to get out of bed or when we look romantically to the years before kids, craving the allure of freedom instead of this daily tiredness and responsibility. He does not abandon us when we turn on the TV because we have no words in our bodies left to offer to our children. He loves us. He is steadfast in love and mercy. In the midst of great sorrow and grief, we can find comfort in the constant love of God.

When we feel sad or empty, we can encourage our hearts to find hope in Christ, our Savior and our God (Psalm 42:11). God will send His faithful love to us both today and for all eternity (verse 8). And one day, Jesus will come again to restore all things (Revelation 21). There will be no more sadness or crying. Christ will be our light, and we will see Him face to face (Revelation 21:23). All will be right.

So if you feel despair today, turn to the Lord and find hope in Jesus because He cares for you. When your emotions feel absent or unstable, find rest in God, depending on His faithful love for you in every season (verse 8). And though it may require extra strength from you, talk to yourself. Remind yourself of what is true, and press into the Word of God, even in the darkness. As we fix our eyes on Jesus, we know that God is holding us. He will never let us go, even in our seasons of sadness.

Resource for further study:
Never Alone: Walking with God through Depression | A Study from The Daily Grace Co.®

"So if you feel despair today, turn to the Lord and find hope in Jesus because He cares for you."

Day 4 Questions

How has despair been evident in your life? What has despair looked like physically, emotionally, and spiritually?

Read Ephesians 1:3-14, 20-23. What truths from these verses could you tell yourself when you feel despair?

One antidote to despair is thankfulness. Spend time thanking the Lord for three blessings of motherhood today.

Today's Notes

ATTRIBUTE OF GOD I AM MEDITATING ON TODAY:

REMEMBER THIS:

WE CAN GO TO JESUS
WHEN WE FEEL LONELY
BECAUSE HE IS OUR
CLOSEST FRIEND.

Day 5

Deuteronomy 31:6
Psalm 25
Matthew 28:20b
—
Practice this week's
memory verse
on page 63.

Loneliness

You are rarely alone. But even as tiny feet pitter-patter around you all day long, you still feel lonely. Even though you are surrounded by little ones every waking second, you feel so alone. You miss adult conversations and going outside without food stains on your shirt.

Maybe because of nap times, sports schedules, or working from home, you have found yourself in a season of isolation. Or maybe you feel lonely because you are different from the other moms around you. You are older than the moms around you, or younger. You work or stay at home, whatever is contrary to the norms of your community. There is no one friend who is just like you—who understands you through and through.

Loneliness is a common experience in life. In different seasons and for different reasons, we can find ourselves isolated from others. But even when no one else is around, we are never truly abandoned. As Christians, we know that we are never truly alone. Even if the whole world leaves us, God is always with us as our closest friend (John 15:15). His friendship is not simply a trite Christian idea to figuratively encourage us through our seasons of loneliness. He is a very real source of comfort and companionship, the One who knows our souls better than anyone else in the world and the One we can talk to day or night.

In today's reading, we see how David, the author of Psalm 25, understood loneliness. As he wrote, he described himself as lonely and afflicted (verse 16). He felt distressed and sad, and there were many enemies pursuing him, trying to hurt him (verse 19). Yet even in his loneliness, he found encouragement in God. He ran to the Lord (verse 1) and remembered that the Lord was with Him. He found hope in the Lord as the One who walked with him and guided him (verses 4–5). David even concluded that the Lord's paths were best for him (verse 10), though they may be lonely from time to time (verse 16).

We all need to be reminded of the Lord's presence and friendship with us. From Scripture, we discover that even mighty kings and great military leaders can feel alone. But just as these men found encouragement in the Lord, so can we. When we feel lonely, we can have hope because God is with us (Deuteronomy 31:6). He is greater than any treasure and any earthly friend, and He will never abandon us (Hebrews 13:5). We can go to Jesus when we feel lonely because He is our closest friend (John 15:15).

At the same time, God made us to be relational beings with those around us. He created local churches in part so that we can be gathered together as families to believers, loving and supporting each other through every season of life (Romans 12:2–4, Hebrews 10:25). Though we may feel tempted to isolate ourselves when we feel different from those around us, God calls us to love one another and press into relationships, especially within our local congregations.

If you are feeling lonely, odds are, another mom around you feels the same way. And amazingly, God can use your current feelings of loneliness for good—to spur you on to love and help other lonely moms around you. Maybe you could be a blessing to another woman as you invite her to coffee or a play date. Maybe you could ask another mom how she is doing in her season of motherhood or ask an older woman for mothering advice. Though it may seem counterintuitive, God can use your season of loneliness to encourage and bless the moms around you as you pursue them in relationships.

Sometimes, though, we can be nervous to initiate relationships. We are scared of rejection or that we will be awkward. But because of the gospel, we can pursue relationships with other women, even if they are not like us. We can initiate get-togethers and face possible rejection because God loves us and has provided every-

thing we need in Christ. We can love others without a sense of neediness because we are completely accepted in Jesus. Even if others do not like us or reciprocate our invitations to be together, God loves us, and He sustains us. Like the psalmist who says, "The LORD is for me; I will not be afraid. What can a mere mortal do to me?" (Psalm 118:6), we can rejoice because we are perfectly whole in Christ. Therefore, we can pursue friendship with others as we live within the freedom of the gospel.

Furthermore, we must recognize that our expectations of friends can sometimes be unrealistic, which causes us to not try at all. We wait for that one special friend who will satisfy all of our relational needs. And at times, God does give us a best friend, someone with whom there is instant chemistry and connection. But even so, no one friend is meant to satisfy our every relational desire. Instead, God sets us in local churches where we can be surrounded by all kinds of women. He provides relationships with different parts of the body of Christ—with those who have different gifts, strengths, and weaknesses than us. Practically, this means that we may have lots of different kinds of friends, and we may have friends who bring out different sides of us. We may have our funny friend who always makes us laugh, our shopping friend, our friend who loves adventures, and our deep-thinking, coffee-date friend. We may have older friends and younger friends, friends who challenge us, and friends we can challenge. As we learn to love people not for what they can give us but for who they are as God's image-bearers, we grow in Christlikeness. Then, we will see each and every friend as an opportunity to love someone as Christ has loved us (Matthew 20:28).

So if you are feeling lonely, draw near to Christ as your closest friend. Pray also that God would provide friends in your local context whom you could love and invest in. Pursue relationships with others, and aim to be a good friend to the women around you. God can use your seasons of loneliness to be a catalyst to grow into greater intimacy with Him and others. He is your closest friend who will never leave you nor forsake you (Matthew 28:20b), and He will provide all you need.

"God can use your seasons of loneliness to be a catalyst to grow into greater intimacy with Him and others."

Day 5 Questions

Read Matthew 11:19. Who did Jesus pursue as His friends on earth?
Did they have it all together?

What qualities do you look for in friends? How could you grow in these
qualities as a friend to others? Who has God put in your life whom you can
pursue this week?

Complete the End-of-Week Reflection on the next page.

End-of-Week Reflection

Think back on all of the Scripture that you read and studied this week as you answer the questions below.

What did you observe about God and His character?

What did you learn about the condition of mankind and yourself?

How did this week's Scripture point to the gospel?

How do the truths you have learned this week about God, man, and the gospel give you hope, peace, and encouragement?

How should you respond to what you read and learned this week? *Write down one or two specific action steps you can take this week to apply what you learned. Then, write a prayer in response to your study of God's Word.*

Week 2 Application

Before we begin a new week of study, take some time to apply
and share the truths of Scripture you learned this week.
Here are a few ideas of how you could do this:

Meet Up

Schedule a meet-up with a friend to share what you are learning
from God's Word.

Worship

Spend time worshiping God in a way that is meaningful to you, whether that is
taking a walk in nature, painting, drawing, singing, etc.

Pray

Use these prompts to journal or pray through what God is revealing to you
through your study of His Word.

- *Lord, I feel . . .*

- *Lord, You are . . .*

- *Lord, forgive me for . . .*

- *Lord, help me with . . .*

Paraphrase

Paraphrase the Scripture you read this week.

Dig Deeper

Use a study Bible or commentary to help you answer questions that came up as you read this week's Scripture.

Take Action

Take steps to fulfill the action steps you listed on Day 5.

Highlight

Use highlighters to mark the places you see the metanarrative of Scripture in one or more of the passages that you read this week. (See "The Metanarrative of Scripture" on page 15.)

"Christian women cannot learn mothering from talk-show hosts, magazine articles at the checkout stand, or classes on self-esteem. A healthy, godly view of mothering must be learned from the Scriptures."

Nancy Wilson

(SPROUL 2001, 55)

Biblical Hope for Our Difficult Emotions

Part 2

Week 3 Introduction

This week, we will discuss five additional difficult emotions in motherhood: discontentment, impatience, self-pity, feelings of failure, and the struggle for control. Even though we can experience these emotions, the Lord can use our struggles to strengthen our faith and grow our character.

Below are a few ideas to keep in mind as you begin this week's study:

We can be content in the Lord, even when life does not go as we planned.

Our identity and worth are secure in Christ.

God's grace is sufficient. Though we will fail, God lavishes us with grace and supplies us with the strength we need every day.

As you prepare for this week of the study, pray that you would look to the Lord, finding your worth not in what you do but in Christ. Pray that a love for God would compel you to love your children well. Reflect also on the following questions:

When are you most tempted toward discontentment, self-pity, or feelings of failure in your mothering?

How has impatience been prevalent in your parenting?

When life feels out of control, how do you typically respond?

MEMORY VERSE

Philippians 2:3

Do nothing out of selfish
ambition or conceit, but in
humility consider others as more
important than yourselves.

OUR SOULS WERE
MADE TO FIND
CONTENTMENT IN
THE LORD.

Day 1

2 Corinthians 12:9–10
Philippians 4:11–13

—

Practice this week's
memory verse
on page 103.

Discontentment

As moms, we often live for the next season of life. We want a different stage of parenting, thinking:

When my baby finally sleeps through the night, then I'll be happy...

When she is finally potty trained, then I can relax...

When he is finally of school age and out of the house for a few hours, then I'll be content...

When they can finally drive themselves to school, then life will be good...

Or maybe, you feel discontent as you look at the women around you. You compare yourself, thinking, *If only I had her husband. Her life looks so easy. If only I was as financially stable, beautiful, skinny, or organized as that other mom...*

But as we soon discover, even when we reach the "finish line" of what we have deemed necessary for happiness, we are still unhappy. Nothing truly changes. Although we experience momentary relief when our babies finally sleep through the night, we quickly replace one goal with another. Soon after we regain sleep, we notice that there are still so many diapers to change. We remember that diapers are so expensive, and we recall how much it disrupts our days to stop and change diapers every hour. *If only she were potty-trained*, we think. *Then life would really be good.* Instead of permanently dwelling in thankfulness for the current blessing of a sleeping child, we are quickly off to the next goal, expecting that it will bring the relief and joy our souls crave.

Our real problem is not that our child woke up teething or that our teenager is withdrawing from us. Our problem with discontentment is that we look to the world or to the circumstances around us to make us happy. Truthfully, this world is broken. Life is hard, and there are always reasons to be discontent. Because we live in a fallen world, our bodies ache. We lose our tempers. Our children misbehave. We are inconvenienced, bothered, and sinned against. Whenever we expect someone or something to make us happy, we will be disappointed.

Contrary to the messaging of popular culture, true contentment is not rooted in our circumstances. It is not found in the amount of items we own or in the behavior of our children. Our contentment, as Christians, is rooted in Christ. We have everything we need to be content because Jesus is enough for us, and He satisfies our souls.

The Apostle Paul wrote about contentment while he was in prison. He said, "I have learned to be content in whatever circumstances I find myself. I know how to make do with little, and I know how to make do with a lot" (Philippians 4:11–12). Paul had learned the secret of true contentment—whether hungry or full, needy or well-supplied. He learned that contentment is not based on anything this world has to offer—whether abundant or lacking—it is rooted in Christ (Philippians 4:13).

It is a dreamy ideal, isn't it? The thought that we could be stable and secure emotionally no matter what happens to us in the day sounds wonderful. As moms, a lot of us are fueled by a roller coaster of our ever-changing emotions. If our days are productive, our children behave, and we feel a sense of ineffable happiness, life is good. If we wake up late, the car will not start, or it is a tight month financially, life is bad. Even if one day is wonderful, there is no guarantee that the next day will be. Thankfully, Paul offers us another way.

In Philippians 4, Paul says that he has learned contentment in any and every circumstance because of Christ. This means that when we remember Jesus—how He not only saved us but also redeemed us (Ephesians 1:3–10) and how He adopted us as His children, offering us an eternal inheritance (Ephesians 1:11)—our perspectives change. When we remember that God controls all, determining our every step and every breath, our contentment despite the inconveniences of life grows. Even when we face troubles, we can rejoice in our weaknesses. For when we are weak, Christ is strong (2 Corinthians 12:9–10). As we look to Christ, we rejoice in any and every situation because He has forgiven us of our sins, saved us from darkness, and brought us to light. He will supply all we need for each day. He is enough for us, no matter what the day may bring.

When we look to others to make us happy, we expect them to fill us in ways that they were never meant to do. Instead of making us happy, they become sources of slavery for us. As Tim Keller said in his study on Galatians, "If anything but Jesus is a requirement for being happy or worthy, that thing will become our slavemaster" (Keller 2003, 99). If that thing (or he or she) controls our happiness, we become victims of its whims, giving it the keys to our happiness. Instead, Jesus has given us everything we need in Himself. His love for us is stable and secure. As we fall in love with Jesus, we discover that all the things we expect to satisfy us do not truly satisfy. Our souls were made to find contentment in the Lord. We can be fully satisfied in Him. Nothing else compares.

"We have everything we need to be content because Jesus is enough for us, and He satisfies our souls."

Day 1 Questions

What do you think you need to be happy? How does today's reading change your perspective?

Read Habakkuk 3:17–19. Make your own list of desires. Then, like the author of Habakkuk, commit that even if the fig tree does not blossom, or even if your desires do not come to pass, you will rejoice in the Lord.

Look up the song "It Is Well with My Soul." Sing the hymn back to the Lord today, affirming that no matter what the day brings, the Lord is enough for you.

Today's Notes

ATTRIBUTE OF GOD I AM MEDITATING ON TODAY:

REMEMBER THIS:

"It Is Well with My Soul"

HORATIO G. SPAFFORD, C. 1876

When peace like a river attendeth my way,
when sorrows like sea billows roll,
whatever my lot, Thou hast taught me to say,
"It is well, it is well with my soul."

Though Satan should buffet, though trials should come,
let this blest assurance control:
that Christ has regarded my helpless estate,
and has shed His own blood for my soul.

My sin—oh, the bliss of this glorious thought!
My sin, not in part, but the whole,
is nailed to the cross, and I bear it no more;
praise the Lord, praise the Lord, O my soul!

And Lord, haste the day when my faith shall be sight,
the clouds be rolled back as a scroll;
the trump shall resound and the Lord shall descend;
even so, it is well with my soul.

It is well with my soul;
it is well, it is well with my soul!

GOD CALLS US TO
GROW IN PATIENCE
BECAUSE HE HAS BEEN
PATIENT WITH US.

Day 2

Proverbs 14:29
Proverbs 15:18
Proverbs 16:32
Ephesians 4:1–3
—
Practice this week's
memory verse
on page 103.

Impatience

Do your children regularly test your patience? Even today, perhaps your kids took too long to put on their shoes. You felt your heart rate rise as you tried to hold your tongue and wait patiently. But inwardly, you complained, *Don't they know I'm already running late?* Or maybe your child is easily distracted. Every time she shares a story, you groan internally because each story takes so long. *Can't she just focus on her words and get to the point?* You want to be patient, but it is a real struggle.

Sometimes, our battles against impatience are because of trivial frustrations throughout the day. Other times, our patience is tested because of more severe problems. Maybe for years, your child has abandoned his responsibilities. But now, he is skipping class, hanging out with the wrong crowd, and frustratingly neglecting to pick up his clothes until there is literally no more walking space in his room. You have tried to be patient in your parenting, but you just want him to change, now. Or worse, your child has been walking away from the Lord for the past few years, and you eagerly yearn for her to be right with God. It takes everything within you to wait patiently on the Lord.

If there is anything we know as moms, it is that our patience will be tested through the fires of motherhood. Even so, God promises to use each and every stressful situation to grow our faith and remind us of His power, sovereignty, and love.

Before we dive into today's reading, let us honestly evaluate how we are in this area. When your patience is threatened, how do you respond?

Take a moment to process the above question before you turn the page.

Often, we want to be patient as moms. When provoked, we try to muster up patience from deep within ourselves, but we feel stuck—like life must keep running at an Olympic speed, with every second having a scheduled purpose. We simply do not have time in our busy schedules for the mistakes of our children. So when our children mess up our plans and we feel our patience being stretched thin, we forcibly take a deep breath and respond either with anger, lashing out against our children, or with stress, internalizing our impatience until pimples break out on our faces and our backs grow tight. We may even try to manipulate our children by lying to or shaming them until they begin to move according to our timelines. We count to ten and practice breathing exercises, but inwardly, our hearts rage with impatience. And on some days, we give up altogether. Like a nursing baby who wakes from her contented sleep only to instantly erupt in a DEFCON 1 screech of hunger, we just as quickly lose our patience. In frustration, we hope: *there has to be a better way.*

Thankfully, the gospel changes the way we parent in all ways, including how we respond to moments of stress and interruption. In today's reading, we looked at several proverbs about patience, and it is a good reminder for us as moms. According to Scripture, "Patience is better than power, and controlling one's emotions, than capturing a city" (Proverbs 16:32). Though we may try to gain control over our children through anger or manipulation, God reminds us that patience is the better way. Indeed, our impatience and quick tempers in situations

actually make the problem worse, not better (Proverbs 15:18). Within these verses, we see that patience is not simply an admirable ideal to put on our wishlists; it is a command of God in light of His grace for us (Ephesians 4:1–3).

But as we have discussed, simply mustering up the willpower to grow in patience does not often work. We try to be patient as moms, but we fail over and over again, feeling regular shame and regret. So how do we grow in this area? We can grow in patience by meditating on the life of Christ and by dwelling on God's patience with us.

When we look at the life of Christ, we see practical examples of how Jesus modeled patience to those who were around Him. Throughout His life, Jesus was regularly interrupted (Matthew 8:28–34, 14:13–14). While traveling, He was often surrounded by people who would track Him down, seeking His blessings or wisdom (Matthew 9:1–26). Even so, He modeled perfect patience, knowing that these interruptions were not accidents. They were sovereignly ordained opportunities to love the people around Him.

In the same way, our inconveniences and stresses within motherhood are not accidents. They are divine opportunities to love our children and grow in the fruit of the Spirit—in love, patience, and self-control (Galatians 5:22–23). God controls our days, and every single one of our moments is perfectly planned by the Lord for our growth and sanctification. Even the loudest and most inconvenient toddler tantrum is under the sovereign hand of

God. Nothing surprises Him, and nothing is outside of His reach.

Therefore, in light of God's sovereignty, we can rest even when our days do not go according to plan. After all, our worth is not found in keeping a perfectly ideal schedule. Instead, sometimes the best thing that we can do is stop our regularly scheduled programming to sit with our children, give them a hug, help them with an unplanned problem, or read them a book. God does not want us to be so rigid with our schedules that we miss the opportunities He places before us to love our children. These are the opportunities He designed for us to love them.

Not only this, but God calls us to grow in patience because He has been patient with us (Ephesians 4:1–3, 2 Peter 3:9). Though we mess up, over and over again, God patiently draws us to Himself. He loves us, corrects us in gentleness, and teaches us. He does not impatiently tap his toes and point at His watch condescendingly when we do not run at top speed. He is patient with us. In fact, it is His kindness, not His impatience, that leads us to repentance (Romans 2:4). Because of God's patience with us, we now can be patient with others too.

Even in stressful moments, we have the opportunity to be amazed at the Lord's patience with us and to grow in our patience with our children, being humbled when we fall short and turning to the Lord with repentance and faith when we fail. Instead of viewing parenting interruptions as unholy inconveniences, we know: interruptions are opportunities. Let us use these divine opportunities to trust God and love our children today.

"In light of God's sovereignty, we can rest even when our days do not go according to plan."

Day 2 Questions

Read 2 Peter 3:9. Reflect on the Lord's patience with you, and pray that the Lord would grow your patience.

How can you create more margin in your day to be available for life's interruptions? Are there any activities that you should cut?

Think about the last time you lost your patience as a mom. Have you confessed your sin to the Lord and to your child? What would it look like for you to respond patiently next time?

Today's Notes

ATTRIBUTE OF GOD I AM MEDITATING ON TODAY:

REMEMBER THIS:

SERVE YOUR FAMILY
WITH JOY, KNOWING
THAT GOD SEES IT ALL.

Self-Pity

Have you ever thought the following?

No one appreciates everything I do for my family. My kids aren't grateful for all I do for them. My husband doesn't even notice how I take care of the house each week or how I filled up his gas tank or how I helped the kids with their homework. He thinks he can just relax and watch TV, and I'll take care of everything else, but I have so much to do! I've surrendered everything for my family, and no one even notices!

Feelings of self-pity can easily creep into motherhood. The harder we work, the more tempting it can be to feel dissatisfied when others do not affirm our sacrifices. We can easily develop a martyr complex or a victim mentality, subconsciously thinking, *When we work hard for our families, no one notices. What's the point of it all, anyway?*

Not only this, but our feelings of self-pity are often culturally affirmed. In this world, we are taught that everything must be equal. If household duties are not split fifty-fifty, we should demand that things change. If we serve our families without receiving the appropriate affirmation, we should speak up for "our needs" and defend "our rights." But as we see in Philippians 2, Scripture offers a new paradigm for serving others. Our service to others is no longer based on the worthiness of those whom we serve. It is not even dependent on the gratitude of our families. Instead, we serve others because Christ has served us.

Paul, who is writing the book of Philippians from prison, encourages his readers to find joy and worth in Jesus alone—not in their résumés, the statuses of their families, or in any deed they have done for the Lord (Philippians 3:1–7). Paul says that if we have truly experienced the love of Christ, it will change our entire lives, including how we love and serve those around us (Philippians 2:1–4).

In today's verses, Paul encourages us to consider the life of Jesus. Though Jesus was living in the perfection of heaven with no need of anything, He came near, surrendering His kingly rights in order to reconcile us to the Father. Though He was God, He humbled Himself, taking on human flesh (verse 7). He experienced aches and pains, boo-boos and bruises—skin that could be torn and bones that could be broken. But even more than this, He humbled Himself to the point of death, taking on our sins and enduring the punishment we deserve, dying on the cross for us (verse 8). Now, because of His faithful sacrifice, God has exalted Jesus above every name in heaven and on earth (verse 9). And one day, every knee will bow, and every tongue will confess that Jesus is the Lord (verses 10–11).

Isn't that powerful? Though we could do nothing to earn Christ's love and favor, He has given them to us freely. Though we were guilty and condemned in our sins, ungrateful and unworthy, Jesus died for us (Romans 5:8). Truly, Jesus is our example of how we are to love our families.

Realistically, our families will never understand every sacrifice we have made on their behalf. But in a strange way, we do not do it for them. We do it for Christ. Because Jesus loved us and sacrificed His life for ours, we now joyfully love others, not expecting reciprocity or thankfulness but simply reflecting His love for us. In light of the gospel, we no longer serve our families to get a "thank you." We serve them because God has loved us.

Humbly loving our families brings great joy to the mundane moments of motherhood. For we know that through every season, Christ is with us, and He sees our every sacrifice. He sees every nose you wipe, every pile of laundry you fold, and every grocery run you make. He sees your love for your family, and He is pleased. In light of the gospel, then, we can entrust ourselves to our Creator, while we continue doing good (1 Peter 4:19).

Not only this, but there is great freedom when we learn to love others with the love of Christ. Because of Jesus, we are no longer slaves to the approval and affirmation of others; we have everything we need in Christ. Similarly, humbly serving our families becomes something that is not only good for our souls—as we count others more important than ourselves (verse 3) and prioritize their interests above our own (verse 4)—but it is also helpful for our families, who are no longer buried under the burdens and expectations of our self-martyrdom. It brings freedom both to us and to our families.

At the same time, if you are married, honest communication with your spouse is very important. Be careful not to let bitterness grow in your heart (Hebrews 12:15). If there are patterns that need to be adjusted or family rhythms that should be changed, humbly talk to your spouse to find a solution. If you feel like your husband is not helping enough around the house, gently have a conversation with him, not in a spirit of condemnation but with a heart of unity and love.

Ultimately, when you serve your family to the glory of God, you are serving the Lord. He sees every sacrifice you make for your family. Therefore, do not grow weary in doing good (Galatians 6:9). Instead, serve your family with joy, knowing that God sees it all.

"Humbly loving our families brings great joy to the mundane moments of motherhood."

Day 3 Questions

How have you allowed bitterness and self-pity to creep into your motherhood?

Reflect on a recent instance where you succumbed to self-pity. What did you hope your family would give you (affirmation, love, worth, or support)? How is this need satisfied in Christ?

Read Colossians 1:15–20 and spend time in prayer, thanking Jesus for all He has done for you. How does a proper view of Christ change the way you serve your family?

Today's Notes

ATTRIBUTE OF GOD I AM MEDITATING ON TODAY:

REMEMBER THIS:

Teaching Your Children About God

As Christian moms, we are called to teach our children about the Lord. It is an incredible opportunity to raise our children in the faith. And as Deuteronomy 6:7–9 says, we can do this at all times, whether sitting in our houses or walking along the road. In every season, we can impart a biblical worldview and teach our children about the beauty of God.

If you do not know where to begin, consider one of the following activities:

- Keep it simple! Pick a regular time, such as during breakfast or at bedtime, to teach your children about God. Sing a song, read a Bible story, and talk about it together.

- Open your favorite book of the Bible and start reading the Scriptures with your child. Ask them "what happened" in the passage, and talk about what the verses mean together.

- After church, talk about what you learned during the sermon.

- Reach out to a local mom from your church and ask for advice in discipling your children.

- Read a Christian Bible study or resource with your child, such as *All About Jesus | A Family Devotional* from The Daily Grace Co.®

- Buy a hymn book and learn the songs together.

- Memorize Scripture with your children, teaching them to treasure God's Word in their hearts.

- Ask your local pastor for help teaching your child about God.

- Look to older women in the faith. Ask for advice on how they raised their children.

- Connect with moms from your local church and do a Bible study together!

"Repeat them to your children. Talk about them when you sit in your house and when you walk along the road, when you lie down and when you get up. Bind them as a sign on your hand and let them be a symbol on your forehead. Write them on the doorposts of your house and on your city gates."

Deuteronomy 6:7-9

FAITHFULNESS,
NOT PERFECTION,
IS OUR GOAL.

Failure

Before you became a mom, what dreams did you have for motherhood? Did you imagine cooking organic meals and gently patting your child's nose with leftover flour from your homemade sourdough bread? Did you imagine a vinyl playing in the background while your children painted neatly at the dining room table? Did you envision happy Christmas mornings—raising thoughtful, thankful, and respectful children who obeyed the first time, were not spoiled, and always said sorry when they messed up? Whatever your dreams of motherhood looked like, you likely experienced a rude awakening when your children came with wills and desires of their own, often directly against yours.

No matter how beautiful our dreams are, because of the fallenness of this world, our picture-perfect moments are not our regular, everyday realities. Our children get moody and sick. We discover that our tiny, beautiful babies are little sinners too. And sometimes, life changes in ways we never could have predicted, pushing directly up against our ideals and dreams.

For example, maybe you and your spouse always wanted to travel the world, but you have not had the opportunity because you had children. Although you are thrilled to be a mom, you experience a sliver of resentment when you see your friends post about the life you imagined. Or maybe you always dreamed of dominating the corporate world, until your life suddenly pivoted because of two pink lines on a stick. Though your priorities immediately changed, you still try to do both—working as if you do not have children and having children as if you do not work. You regularly feel like you are failing in one (or both) of these departments. Now instead of homemade, organic meals, you settle for mac and cheese and dino nuggets. Instead of picture-perfect mornings, your children cry for more toys as milk spills, hormones rage, and your temper rises.

We all fail as moms, missing the mark on both internal and external expectations. We sin, make mistakes, and fail others. Not only this, but we are physically incapable of making everyone happy all of the time. So is there hope for us when we fail, disappointing either ourselves or others?

As we read today, we see that the author of Psalm 130 understands failure. Throughout the psalm, he expresses disappointing circumstances, failures, and even his own sins. He is acutely aware of his need and brokenness. But notice how he responds to feelings of failure. Instead of beating himself up in regret when he fails or trying to solve his problems on his own, he runs to the Lord. He cries out to God from the depths of his despair (verse 1), pleading for the Lord's help, mercy, and forgiveness (verses 2–4). He remembers that though the Lord is righteous and holy, He is also full of forgiveness (verse 4). The psalmist knows that he cannot live life on his own, so he waits upon the Lord (verses 5–6), placing his hope in God alone (verse 7).

In light of this, Psalm 130 provides a helpful model for us to follow when we fail as moms. When we fail, we too can run to God for forgiveness and grace. God does not want us to fix our mistakes on our own or wallow in self-pity. He does not expect us to be perfect moms, nor does He impatiently demand that we run our households with effortless perfection. Rather, He invites us to repent of our sins and cling to His grace, knowing we are completely loved and accepted in Christ. He desires that we come to Him in repentance and faith, trusting in His steadfast love.

This message of grace is incredibly counter-cultural. The world tells us that we have value because of what we do. It tells us that if we accomplish our professional goals and fulfill our personal dreams, we have lived a good life. But the message of Christianity is different. It begins with an acknowledgment of what we are not (Begg 2021, 200). It begins with our need for a Savior because we have fallen short and will never be enough.

Our worth as women is not in our performance or accomplishments as moms. Notably, many heroes of the faith did not have "successful" lives according to worldly standards. They were poor, beaten, and killed, not receiving the things promised (Hebrews 11:13, 35–40). They sinned and failed. The dreams they had for the future were surely not the particular persecutions and troubles they faced. Yet God honored them, not because they were perfect but because of their faith in Christ. We too can find hope and forgiveness, even when we fail, by looking to Christ for mercy. Faithfulness, not perfection, is our goal.

So when we experience a loss of dreams—when life does not look like we expected or we fall short—we can remember our loving, heavenly Savior. Our identities are no longer rooted in what we do or how well we perform. They are secure in Christ. We place our confidence not in our own accomplishments but in the perfection of Christ.

And when our motherhood experience is not what we hoped it would be, when our failures are ever before us or our dreams of old feel like distant realities, we can wait upon the Lord, putting our trust in His steadfast love (Psalm 130:7–8). Our hope is not in perfect Christmas memories nor in flour-dusted noses but in Christ. Nothing can thwart God's good plans for us, including our own mistakes and failures.

In truth, we will fail as moms. But even when we fall short, God never does. He is always perfect and always good. Christ is our perfect righteousness. We can rely on His steadfast love (verse 7).

"We place our confidence not in our own accomplishments but in the perfection of Christ."

Day 4 Questions

In what ways do you feel like a failure as a mom?

Are your reasons for feelings of failure primarily external (falling short of the expectations of others) or internal (failing your own expectations)?

Following the model of Psalm 130, how can you run to the Lord for forgiveness and grace today?

Today's Notes

ATTRIBUTE OF GOD I AM MEDITATING ON TODAY:

REMEMBER THIS:

WHILE WE ARE
NOT IN CONTROL,
GOD IS, AND
HE CAN BE TRUSTED.

Day 5

Psalm 73:23-28
Proverbs 19:21
Galatians 5:22-23
—
Practice this week's
memory verse
on page 103.

Control

Sometimes it is easy to look back on our pre-motherhood life as the "days of control." You could go to the bathroom whenever you wanted, take showers whenever you wanted, and make whatever plans you desired for Saturday mornings. *Oh, the days of bliss.* Now, it may feel like you cannot control anything. You cannot control your children, your weekends, or even your own emotions. Some days, you cannot keep a train of thought because you are constantly interrupted by your toddler's questions. You cannot even control your sleep schedule, though you try. Instead of blissful dreams, you are interrupted by crying babies, bad dreams, and late curfews. Life can feel completely out of control, and you grieve the loss of autonomy and freedom.

Why do we want control, anyway? Often, we want to control our circumstances because we want to make life better (Moore, 2008). When faced with difficulties — from unpredictable nap schedules to feelings of identity loss as moms, we want security. We want the comfort of knowing what is going to happen next. But at times, if we are not careful, we may feel the need to control our circumstances because we do not believe that God will take care of us. We think we could make better plans than God, and we are deceived into believing the lie that with enough careful planning, we determine our futures. When this happens, the desire for control can become a subtle, yet all-consuming, mission.

This quest for control can be so sneaky because, on the one hand, we do have influence in our days. God has given us a dominion mandate to take care of the earth (Genesis 1:28). He has given us authority over the plants and the animals — to shape and steward the world around us for the glory of God. He has also given us authority as moms — to decide what we are having for dinner, what after-school activities our children will participate in, and when bedtime should be. But at times, we confuse authority or influence with absolute control. We conflate ourselves with God, believing that we have more power and responsibility than we actually have (Genesis 3:3–6).

The Bible tells us that there is only one God who rules the universe with His words. We are not God, nor do we have ultimate control over our circumstances (Proverbs 19:21). We cannot control the influence of other people on our children, though we can guard, shape, and protect them. We cannot control how our children will interpret their childhoods, what allergies they will have, or whether they will share our Christian faith. There is so much about our lives and in our mothering that we cannot control. But while we are not in control, God is, and He can be trusted.

In Psalm 73, we see a firsthand example of trusting God when life feels out of control. As the author of the psalm looked around himself, he was furious. He remarked that the wicked thrived on earth, while the righteous suffered. He ranted and raved about his complaints until he remembered the Lord. But when he looked up, he recalled the justice and goodness of God. He remembered that God was with him always as his portion and his good (verses 23–28), and he found comfort and consolation in the Lord's perfect plans.

In the same way, our days of mothering can often remind us that we are not in control. It is easy to look back on the "good ole days" of predictable schedules when life feels hard. But truthfully, even when we could spontaneously leave the house without a diaper bag, stroller, or sippy cups, we were never really in control. We just thought we were. When we thought we could ordain our days, it was only an illusion. It was like our children trying to "catch the ocean" with their sand buckets: impossible.

Just like the psalmist does, we can look to God when life feels out of control. We can remember that God sustains all things, even in our parenting. So when potty training does not go

according to plan or when our child fails their math class, we can remember that God is in control. His plans for us are good. When school is canceled for bad weather or our baby is up all night teething, we know God is not surprised. The Lord sees from an eternal perspective, and He works good through every difficulty (Romans 8:28). He is doing more than we could ever ask or imagine (Ephesians 3:20).

Scripture calls us not to sinfully grasp for control of our circumstances but to instead exercise self-control by placing our trust in God. Importantly, there is a difference between being controlling and exercising self-control. One seeks mastery over external circumstances, while the other seeks mastery over our internal thoughts, wills, and emotions. A person who is self-controlled learns to exercise temperance and say "no" to ungodly desires. The Bible calls us to exercise self-control over our bodies, as we live in ways that honor Christ (1 Thessalonians 5:8). It requires great self-control to trust God in our day-to-day lives. Yet because of the Spirit's work within us (Galatians 5:22–23), we can stand firm in our fight against sin, resisting ungodly urges to manipulate or micromanage our circumstances because we trust that God has good plans for us.

The fact that we are not in control of our circumstances is actually good news for the Christian because we know the One who is in control, and He is good. The Lord holds our hands and leads us to glory (Psalm 73:23–24). Even though everyone else may fail us, including our very selves, He is for us (Romans 8:31). He provides for us, and we can trust Him. He is our portion and all that we need (Psalm 73:26). He is the good and just God who planned our days before we were even born (Psalm 139:16, Ephesians 1:4–6).

Truthfully, we are not in control of tomorrow, just as we are not in control of our next breath, but we know the One who is (Isaiah 46:10), and He does what is best. We can experience security and comfort when we remember that God loves us, and He will take care of us.

"Scripture calls us not to sinfully grasp for control of our circumstances but to instead exercise self-control by placing our trust in God."

Day 5 Questions

How do you struggle for control throughout your mothering days?

In light of Galatians 5:22–23, what would it look like for you to live a self-controlled — not controlling — life?

Complete the End-of-Week Reflection on the next page.

End-of-Week Reflection

Think back on all of the Scripture that you read and studied this week
as you answer the questions below.

What did you observe about God and His character?

What did you learn about the condition of mankind and yourself?

How did this week's Scripture point to the gospel?

How do the truths you have learned this week about God, man, and the gospel give you hope, peace, and encouragement?

How should you respond to what you read and learned this week? *Write down one or two specific action steps you can take this week to apply what you learned. Then, write a prayer in response to your study of God's Word.*

Week 3 Application

Before we begin a new week of study, take some time to apply
and share the truths of Scripture you learned this week.
Here are a few ideas of how you could do this:

Meet Up

Schedule a meet-up with a friend to share what you are learning
from God's Word.

Worship

Spend time worshiping God in a way that is meaningful to you, whether that is
taking a walk in nature, painting, drawing, singing, etc.

Pray

Use these prompts to journal or pray through what God is revealing to you
through your study of His Word.

- *Lord, I feel . . .*

- *Lord, You are . . .*

- *Lord, forgive me for . . .*

- *Lord, help me with . . .*

Paraphrase

Paraphrase the Scripture you read this week.

Dig Deeper

Use a study Bible or commentary to help you answer questions that came up as you read this week's Scripture.

Take Action

Take steps to fulfill the action steps you listed on Day 5.

Highlight

Use highlighters to mark the places you see the metanarrative of Scripture in one or more of the passages that you read this week. (See "The Metanarrative of Scripture" on page 15.)

"It is natural to quarrel, to be selfish, to live a small-minded life. It is supernatural to love unconditionally, to serve others, to live a life of vision and faith."

Sally Clarkson

(2015)

Biblical Hope
for Our
Difficult Emotions

Part 3

Week 4 Introduction

During this week of the study, we will be discussing five additional emotional experiences in motherhood: exhaustion, jealousy, dissatisfaction, laziness, and overwhelming busyness. Through every emotion, we discover that God is both holy—perfect and worthy of worship—and tender with us. He is near to the weary and brokenhearted.

This week, we will dwell especially on the following truths:

When we are overwhelmed and exhausted, we can look to Christ for rest.	Knowing and enjoying Christ is our greatest purpose in life.	God has supplied everything we need in Himself.

As you prepare for this week, pray that the Lord would be your strength in the midst of the tiring days of motherhood. Pray that God would give you wisdom as you make decisions and contentment as you look to Him. Reflect also on the following questions before you begin this week's content:

In what season were you the most exhausted as a mom? How was the Lord gracious to you in that season?	How would you like to grow in contentment in this season of motherhood?	Do you tend to struggle more with laziness or overwhelming busyness? What does this look like for you?

MEMORY VERSE

2 Corinthians 9:8

And God is able to make
every grace overflow to you,
so that in every way, always
having everything you need,
you may excel in every
good work.

GOD KNOWS
YOUR EXHAUSTION,
AND HE OFFERS
TO SUSTAIN YOU.

Day 1

Isaiah 40:9-11,
28-31
—
Practice this week's
memory verse
on page 145.

Exhaustion

You are tired. You are just *so* tired. As soon as your alarm clock rings, you think, *I don't want to do today*. It has been months, years even, since you felt rejuvenated. Each day leaves you feeling depleted, discouraged, and tired. You are exhausted from the start to the finish of the day.

Truthfully, motherhood is tiring. Every day, we pour out our lives for the sake of our children. There is no time off for moms. We are mothers 24/7, regularly putting our children's needs before our own. It is easy to grow weary. Yet in your exhaustion, hear God's invitation to you today. Jesus calls you to "Come to [Him], all of you who are weary and burdened, and [He] will give you rest . . . you will find rest for your souls. For [His] yoke is easy and [His] burden is light" (Matthew 11:28–30).

In your tiredness, Jesus does not look down at you, pointing out all the little crumbs still hiding underneath your dining room table. He does not raise His nose at you, criticizing all the laundry left undone. He does not abandon you when you are not running at top speed or condemn you for being tired. He does not expect you to do it all. Instead, He invites you to come and find rest in Him. He is compassionate toward the weary and hurting. He knows that you are tired, and He offers you His strength.

As we talked about during week 1, God is strong when we are weak. Our Creator is infinite in power and strength (Isaiah 40:10). He never gets tired or weary, and He is never confused (verse 28). He does not need sleep because His energy is endless. Yet even with God's infinite strength and power, He is also gentle with us. As Isaiah says, "He tends his flock like a shepherd: He gathers the lambs in his arms and carries them close to his heart; he gently leads those that have young" (verse 11, NIV). The God of unfathomable power is unimaginably tender toward us in our weakness and vulnerability.

Today's verses remind us of the Lord's gentle and purposeful restoration of us in our weakness (Isaiah 40:31). Our Father carefully renews and restores those who trust in Him. He provides the strength and grace we need to endure with faith. As the verses explain, the Lord is the One who renews our strength—not girls' nights, nap time, or the promise of future self-care. Though healthy rhythms such as going to bed on time or scheduling our days can be a means of grace to help us in our mothering, they are not enough. The quick fixes of watching television or browsing social media do not truly satisfy our souls. The Lord deeply and completely renews our lives. We can look to Him for help, remembering that His strength is sufficient for us.

So if you are tired today, run to Jesus. Fall on Him, and remember the Lord's grace and mercy toward you today. When you fall into exhaustion as Isaiah describes (verse 30), overwhelmed by the responsibilities of today, look to Christ for strength, knowing that He will renew you. And as you continue to press into your duties as mom, wait upon the Lord (verse 31), asking for His strength. Pray to God, and ask Him to help you be faithful in your responsibilities of motherhood today.

The beauty of prayer is that we can pray at all times and in every season. We can pray short prayers of, "Help me, Lord!" when the alarm clock goes off, and we can ask for His mercy when we are going to bed. We can pray while we are doing the dishes and when we are changing diapers. We can ask for His help anytime, anywhere.

Sometimes, God may answer our prayers for help through greater endurance, and sometimes He answers them through the support of our local churches. You do not need to go through motherhood alone. The Lord has designed the local church to be a support system for the Christian, a place where you can be known and loved. So as you are able, look to your church, and ask for help from your spouse, a babysitter, or other moms.

But most importantly, the Lord is with you every step of the way. Even with the help and support of your community, there is a level of tiredness that may remain in your motherhood. Biblical motherhood requires self-sacrifice, and parenting can be tiring, even with a village of support. Even so, God sees all the ways you love your children, and He is honored when you continue to endure in faithful, loving mothering. Every sacrifice you make as unto the Lord is counted as worship and is of eternal significance.

As you pour yourself out for the needy, the Lord renews your light and gives you the strength you need (Isaiah 58:10). So do not grow weary in doing good (Galatians 6:9), but press into your biblical responsibilities with wisdom, depending on the strength the Lord provides (Colossians 1:29). As you do, remember the Lord's Word for you today: God knows your exhaustion, and He offers to sustain you. God knows the joys and burdens that come with motherhood, and He offers you His grace in the midst of your weakness (2 Corinthians 12:9). He is sympathetic with you, and He is strong enough to carry you. We can find rest, even when we have an unending to-do list, because we know that God holds the universe together (Colossians 1:17). We do not. He sustains the world. We do not. We do not need to do it all. Indeed, we cannot.

In light of this, the familiar children's lullaby reminds us of a profound truth today: "Jesus loves me—this I know, for the Bible tells me so; Little ones to Him belong. They are weak, but He is strong" (Warner, 1859). Jesus loves you, and He is strong. He will carry you through this season.

"Every sacrifice you make as unto the Lord is counted as worship and is of eternal significance."

Day 1 Questions

Read Ephesians 6:18. What would it look like to remain alert and pray for the Lord's help throughout your days?

When do you feel especially weak or tired in your mothering? Who could you ask for help, possibly within your local church or family?

Spend time praying for the Lord to help you and give you strength in your motherhood.

Today's Notes

ATTRIBUTE OF GOD I AM MEDITATING ON TODAY:

REMEMBER THIS:

THE LORD'S OPINION
OF US MATTERS MOST,
AND HE APPROVES OF US
FULLY IN CHRIST.

Day 2

1 Corinthians 4:3
2 Corinthians
10:1–18
Philippians 4:8
—
Practice this week's
memory verse
on page 145.

Comparison

Comparison can take many forms in motherhood. Maybe you look at another mom and think, *Her life is so much better than mine. Her children are better behaved. They're smarter. They're more self-controlled. They're simply... better.* Or perhaps you compare your life with another mom's belongings, abilities, or relationships. You measure your life compared to hers and are jealous, concluding, *Her car is better than mine. She cooks better than me. Her husband is more attentive and attractive than mine.* Sometimes, your comparisons may even come in the form of self-righteousness. Whether regarding vaccination decisions or TV time convictions, you judge those who make different choices than you do. You compare yourself in millions of ways to the moms around you.

We can often be tempted to look around us in our mothering, fueled by insecurity or pride. But as we quickly realize, the path of comparison is dangerous. When we compare ourselves with others, our joy is quickly dashed. We may feel happy with our lives for a moment...until we see the accomplishments of another child. Then, we suddenly feel insecure and unsatisfied, jealous of the success of another family. We become distracted and self-focused, longing for someone else's life. Our sin of jealousy is joined by a number of other sins, including discontentment, pride, and despair. Yet Scripture calls us to think differently. In today's verses, Paul reminds us not to define our worth according to how we compare with others but rather to look to the Lord and boast in Him.

Throughout 1 and 2 Corinthians, Paul regularly spoke on the topics of comparison and jealousy. The church in Corinth routinely chased after ungodly goals, placing their worth in worldly success and accolades. In the same way, they regularly compared Paul to other leaders and questioned his authority because he was not as politically desirable as other men. In a culture that prioritized beauty and skill, Paul was a tentmaker with a thorn in his flesh (Acts 18:3, 2 Corinthians 12:7). According to the Greek definitions of success, Paul was not outstanding (Barnett 1988, 161).

Even so, Paul did not base his identity on what others thought about him. He did not even care about how he viewed himself. Paul cared about Christ's opinion of him (1 Corinthians 4:3). As a result, Paul did not boast in himself but in God. He knew that the gospel was hidden in jars of clay, and he considered himself to be like a fragile, weak jar containing an invaluable treasure (2 Corinthians 4:1–12). As author Jay Adams describes, "It is interesting to note Paul's attitude toward himself as he engaged in ministry: the treasure was everything; the vessel that contained it, nothing" (Adams 2020, 132). Even when the church again judged Paul and compared him against an unnamed rival, Paul reminded himself (and the church) that he lived for the Lord, not man (2 Corinthians 10). He knew that jealousy and comparisons were futile and ungodly endeavors.

As Christian moms, we find a challenging but important reminder in Paul's writings. Paul's words remind us that our worth as women is not found in our relationships, capabilities, or belongings. It is not in how we rank compared to other moms. Our worth is firmly rooted in the Lord.

Through the gospel, God has given us new identities and priorities (2 Corinthians 5:17). The Lord is the hero of our stories, and He has given us abundant blessings in Christ (Ephesians 1:3). Our worth is no longer limited to how beautiful our children's hair is on picture day or who brought the best teacher appreciation gift. It is firmly rooted in what Jesus has done for us. When we look to Jesus, we find an eternal joy and quiet settledness that cannot be disrupted. We find comfort not in our accomplishments but in Christ's.

As a result, we are called to boast not in ourselves but in the Lord. When we feel insecure, wanting to know how we "measure up" to others, God does not call us to look inward—finding our worth in our own abilities as moms as expert hair-braiders or precise bed-makers. Nor does He call us to look outward, determining our identities by comparing our status to others. He calls us to look to Christ.

But how can we remember to boast in the Lord when we are tempted to compare ourselves with others? We must regularly renew our thoughts through time spent in the Word. Instead of dwelling on comparisons and consistently meditating on how we are better or worse than others, we are to think about the hope, love, and joy of Christ. Rather than fueling our discontentment on the fires of comparison, we can give thanks to the Lord for His blessings to other women and in our own lives. We can think about what is pure, lovely, admirable, true, noble, and right, renewing our minds with the truths of God's Word (Philippians 4:8, Romans 12:2). As we do, we are reminded that our worth is secure in Christ. Instead of pursuing a frantic and unstable validation in others, we remember that we have all we need in Christ.

When we take our eyes off of others and fix them on Christ, we realize that the Lord's opinion of us matters most, and He approves of us fully in Christ. And as we make our boast in the Lord, we are able to joyfully follow Him. We are free to serve Christ with greater zeal when we remember our true value is secure in the Lord, and He provides everything we need. We are no longer imprisoned by the opinions of others, living for their approval. Instead, we are satisfied in God, living for Him.

We do not need to look to the right or to the left as moms, fearfully comparing our lots with the women around us. Through the gospel, we are free to be faithful to the life God has called us to. Let us, then, not boast in ourselves but in the treasure of the gospel, hidden in jars of clay.

"Paul's words remind us that our worth as women is not found in our relationships, capabilities, or belongings. It is not in how we rank compared to other moms. Our worth is firmly rooted in the Lord."

Day 2 Questions

Read 1 Samuel 16:7 and Micah 6:6–8. What does the Lord prioritize, and how do these values compare with yours?

How are you tempted to find your worth and identity in your mothering? Is it in your children's performance, your housekeeping abilities, or the items you own? Ask God to reorient your priorities according to a godly perspective in light of 1 Peter 2:9 and Colossians 3:1–3.

Make a thankfulness list of the Lord's blessings to you below. Spend time in prayer, boasting in the Lord's work in your life.

Today's Notes

ATTRIBUTE OF GOD I AM MEDITATING ON TODAY:

REMEMBER THIS:

WE ARE NOT CALLED
TO COMPLAIN BUT
RATHER TO BE THANKFUL
IN ALL CIRCUMSTANCES.

Day 3

Philippians 2:14-16
1 Thessalonians
5:16-18
—
Practice this week's
memory verse
on page 145.

Dissatisfaction

Have you ever complained about your children? Maybe your complaints sound something like, *My kids are so loud. They never pick up after themselves. I just can't take it anymore! They're so reckless and disrespectful.* Or perhaps your complaints surface when you remember your pre-kid life: *Everything was easier when I didn't have kids...*

If there was a microphone to our thoughts, broadcasting our hidden complaints to the outside world, many of us would be horrified. Our internal dialogues reveal dissatisfaction, bitterness, entitlement, and frustration. We are not models of patient motherhood. Instead, we constantly complain when our days do not go our way.

Yet Scripture is clear on the command to not complain. Today's verses specifically tell us not to grumble or complain so that we may be lights in the world, blameless and innocent as children of God (Philippians 2:14–15). We regularly do the opposite. If the line is too long at the grocery store, we complain. If our children do not behave as we want, we complain. Even so, Scripture warns us strongly against the sin of grumbling.

The story of the Israelites is a warning for us about the temptation to complain. In Exodus 16, when the Israelites were in the wilderness, they grumbled about their condition. Though God had saved them from harsh slavery under a tyrannical ruler, they complained about what they did not have (Deuteronomy 1:19–35). They doubted that God would take care of them and grumbled against their leaders. They were dissatisfied in the Lord. But Scripture says that when they grumbled against their leaders, they were actually grumbling against God (Exodus 16:8). Not only this but Israel's complaining was counted as a serious sin (Numbers 14). It was considered rebellion against a holy God.

Today, when we place our faith in Jesus, every one of our sins are washed by the blood of Christ, including our sinful complaining. God has forgiven us of every rebellious thought, action, and deed. At the same time, we are now called to live holy lives, which includes what we think about and what we say. Throughout the New Testament, we are specifically warned not to follow the example of the Israelites in their grumbling (1 Corinthians 10:10). We are not called to complain but rather to be thankful in *all* circumstances.

When we consider the goodness of God in our lives, we realize that there is always something to be thankful for—even when we are frustrated in motherhood by missing socks or lingering crumbs under the dining room table. We can thank the Lord in every season because He is always good to us.

For example, when we are doing laundry and staring down that one lone sock, wondering where its stubborn twin is hiding, we can thank the Lord for the gift of clothes. We can thank God for money to buy socks and for the little feet that wear them. Or, when we are reminded of the crumbs that remain perpetually under our dining room tables, we can thank the Lord for the food we have to feed our children. We can thank God for taste buds that allow us to enjoy our food and that God did not make every meal taste the same. We can thank Him for the texture of food, for the health that allows us to sit together, for a dining table and chairs, and for a family with whom we can enjoy food. We can thank the Lord for cleaning supplies, structure, and order, and that the Lord has given us a family to take care of. We often take the Lord's blessings for granted. Yet in each inconvenience, there is an opportunity to remember the abundant goodness of God.

At the same time, there is a difference between complaining and lamenting. When life does not go our way, when we are tired or frustrated, we can always run to the Lord and talk to Him about it. We can pour out our hearts to Him, knowing that He cares for us. We can ask for our circumstances to change while finding contentment, joy, and hope in His steadfast love. As pastor Rob Brockman describes, "Lament says, 'Confess your anguish. Confess your pain. Lay it out bear!' However, lament then directs us to turn our eyes upon Christ, the many comforts promised to us through the Holy Spirit, and we are reminded of the provision and contentment that comes in Christ!" (Brockman, 2022). The command to not complain does not mean that we ignore our pain or struggles. Rather, it means we run to Christ with them and fall on His mercy. We remember the Lord's care for us, even in our daily frustrations.

But when we do the opposite—when we complain with ungrateful hearts and forget the Lord's mercy—we can look to Christ, the One who covers over every sin. With the help of the Holy Spirit that lives within us, we can change our sinful habits of complaining and redirect our focus onto the goodness of God. Instead of complaining, we can learn to practice gratitude (1 Thessalonians 5:16–18). As Paul models, we can give thanks to the Lord in every situation because contentment is found in God, not in our circumstances (Philippians 4:11–13).

So when you are anxious about tomorrow or frustrated about today, go to Jesus. Remember His abundant goodness to you. Our joy is not rooted in happy, perfect children or a spotless, quiet house. It is rooted in Christ. God has given us everything we need for biblical contentment in Him today.

"With the help of the Holy Spirit that lives within us, we can change our sinful habits of complaining and redirect our focus onto the goodness of God."

Day 3 Questions

Honestly evaluate how regularly you complain about your children. What does your complaining reveal about your heart?

Read 1 Corinthians 10:9-11 and Jude 1:16-21. Compare and contrast a life of faith with a life of unbelief as presented in these verses.

The Israelites in Exodus 16 forgot what God had done for them. Spend time today remembering how the Lord has answered your prayers and thank Him for His blessings to you today.

Today's Notes

ATTRIBUTE OF GOD I AM MEDITATING ON TODAY:

REMEMBER THIS:

Brainstorm: Ways to Connect with Your Children

How would you like to be a more present mom? Sometimes the busyness of life or our own discontentment can distract us from spending quality time with our children. Spend a few minutes now making an intentional plan to engage with your children.

In the spaces provided on these pages, brainstorm a few ways that you could connect with your child.

NAME OF CHILD:_____

YOUR CHILD'S INTERESTS:_____
_____
_____

PLACES, TIMES, AND
OPPORTUNITIES TO CONNECT:
_____
_____
_____

WAYS YOUR CHILD FEELS LOVED:
_____
_____

MAKE A PLAN TO ENGAGE WITH
YOUR CHILD THIS WEEK:_____
_____
_____
_____

NAME OF CHILD:_____

YOUR CHILD'S INTERESTS:_____
_____
_____

PLACES, TIMES, AND
OPPORTUNITIES TO CONNECT:
_____
_____
_____

WAYS YOUR CHILD FEELS LOVED:
_____
_____

MAKE A PLAN TO ENGAGE WITH
YOUR CHILD THIS WEEK:_____
_____
_____
_____

NAME OF CHILD:_____

YOUR CHILD'S INTERESTS:_____
_____
_____

PLACES, TIMES, AND
OPPORTUNITIES TO CONNECT:
_____
_____
_____

WAYS YOUR CHILD FEELS LOVED:
_____
_____

MAKE A PLAN TO ENGAGE WITH
YOUR CHILD THIS WEEK:_____
_____
_____
_____

NAME OF CHILD:_____

YOUR CHILD'S INTERESTS:_____
_____
_____

PLACES, TIMES, AND
OPPORTUNITIES TO CONNECT:
_____
_____
_____

WAYS YOUR CHILD FEELS LOVED:
_____
_____

MAKE A PLAN TO ENGAGE WITH
YOUR CHILD THIS WEEK:_____
_____
_____
_____

OTHER IDEAS:

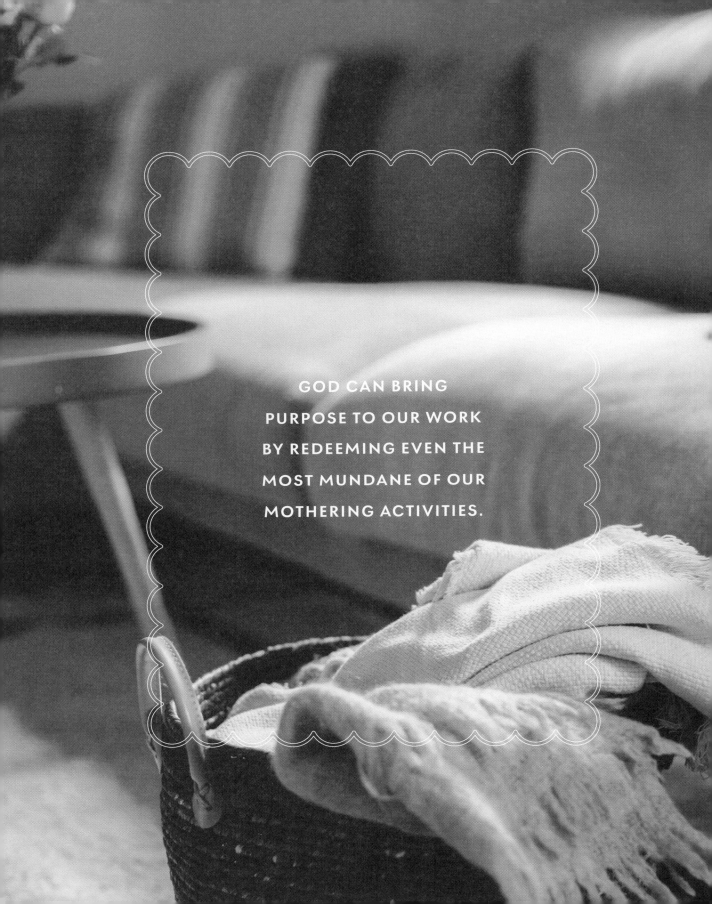

GOD CAN BRING
PURPOSE TO OUR WORK
BY REDEEMING EVEN THE
MOST MUNDANE OF OUR
MOTHERING ACTIVITIES.

Day 4

Proverbs 6:9–11
Proverbs 20:13
Proverbs 31:27
2 Thessalonians 3:6–9
—
Practice this week's
memory verse
on page 145.

Laziness

A Beginning Note: Though many of the examples listed here are geared toward laziness, they can also be indicators of a number of other medical conditions that cause lethargy. If you are experiencing prolonged and unusual fatigue, please contact your doctor.

Do you struggle with laziness in motherhood? Maybe you stacked a pile of books on your bedside table with the good intentions of reading to your children. You even started to read each book…until the novelty wore off. Now, it feels like too much work to read them. Or maybe, instead of regularly engaging with your children, playing games, or finding creative ways to help them grow, you routinely indulge in "just one more minute" on your phone. This habit has likely bled into other areas of your life too. Your sink is full of dirty dishes, and your laundry bin has piled up to the height of an unscalable mountain. You know that you should work harder and be more diligent, but you always seem to come up with another activity that sounds more fun.

We can all struggle with laziness in motherhood from time to time, but our reasons for laziness vary. Sometimes, we have good intentions to engage with our children, but we are easily lulled into the seduction of over-resting. We commit to helping our children with their homework "later," until we become distracted with other activities. Our to-do lists become so long that we give up on our goals altogether and justify, *My kids don't really need help with math. It's probably better if they're self-sufficient and learn it on their own.* We procrastinate our mothering commitments until our promises become nothing more than good-intentioned and unfulfilled wishes.

Other times, we become lazy when we intentionally abscond from our responsibilities. We feel unfulfilled in our roles as moms and choose to prioritize other activities, such as buying new clothes or browsing the internet. We do not like the duties that come with motherhood, so we choose to engage in the activities we prefer instead. Or maybe, we are simply burnt out. After days, months, or years of burning the candle at both ends, we have nothing left. Now, even after a season of healthy healing and recovery, we have chosen to veer toward the other side of the pendulum, choosing to over-rest instead of over-work.

The Bible is clear in its warnings against laziness. As we read today, the book of Proverbs gives many explicit admonitions against it. It says that laziness is not a minor problem or justifiable when met with good intentions. It is a sinful misuse of time that can lead to a number of other sins and consequences, including poverty (Proverbs 13:4), gossip (1 Timothy 5:13), and foolishness (Proverbs 26:16). But contrasted with these warnings, we also read today about another possible path through the life and example of Paul.

Throughout his ministry, Paul worked hard for the glory of God. His life was an example of diligent, faithful hard work (2 Thessalonians 3:6–9). Though Paul could have relied on the generosity of the believers in the towns he visited, he toiled day and night so as not to be a burden to them. He did not attribute his hard work to his personality or preferences. He encouraged believers in his town to do the same, working hard to honor the Lord.

As Christians, we too are called to work hard for the glory of God. As Scripture explains, work is not a bad thing. Work existed before the Fall in the garden of Eden, which means that work, in itself, is not a result of sin (Genesis 2:15). Not only this, but we were created in the image of a working God. As theologian Sinclair Ferguson says, "Twentieth-century man needs to be reminded at times that work is not the result of the Fall. Man was made to work, because the God who made him was a 'working God.' Man was made to be creative, with his mind and his hands. Work is part of the dignity of his existence" (Ferguson 1987, 31).

We were made to work, and thankfully, God has given us work to do. He has designed good deeds for us to do (Ephesians 2:10) and has planned our days with purpose.

When we are lazy, we miss out on the beauty of what God has planned for us. Even so, there is hope for those of us who are stuck in patterns of laziness. When we spend our time poorly, absconding from responsibilities, we can repent, knowing that Jesus is quick to forgive. We can ask for forgiveness and help, knowing that His mercy is greater than all our sins.

Our goal when we repent of laziness is not to become a Terminator-style woman who never rests. Moms need breaks too. Similarly, we are not saved by our "hard work" in mothering. Even the most productive days apart from Christ are futile. Rather, we are saved through Christ's perfect work on the cross. Our goal, then, is to rest in the finished work of Christ while also striving with all our energy to honor Him (Colossians 1:29). We can be faithful in the tasks of today through our faith in Christ, which is expressed through our actions (James 2:14–16).

Thankfully, God can bring purpose to our work by redeeming even the most mundane of our mothering activities. Whether we are putting away winter clothes, folding tiny socks, or carpooling, we can do it all with hearts of worship. For in Christ, we do all things for the glory of God (Colossians 3:23). God encourages us not to grow weary in doing good but to endure with grace, remembering that there will be a reward for us (Galatians 6:6–9).

In faith, we can rest, and we can work, relying on the grace that God supplies. Faithfulness, not perfect productivity, is our aim. The Lord does not want us to overwork, erasing His gifts of grace and rest. Nor does he want us to under-work, neglecting the work He has called us to. Instead, He calls us to be faithful with endurance, living lives that honor Him.

God has given us responsibilities for today. We can be faithful to what the Lord has for us, knowing that He will also supply the grace we need.

"We were made to work, and thankfully, God has given us work to do. He has designed good deeds for us to do (Ephesians 2:10) and has planned our days with purpose."

Day 4 Questions

In what specific ways has the sin of laziness invaded your mothering?

Read 1 Thessalonians 4:11–12 and Ecclesiastes 9:10. What would it look like to use your time well for the glory of God, minding your sphere of influence and working with your own hands?

What is the difference between godly rest and laziness?

Today's Notes

ATTRIBUTE OF GOD I AM MEDITATING ON TODAY:

REMEMBER THIS:

IF YOU ARE IN A SEASON
OF OVERWHELMING
BUSYNESS, PRIORITIZE
YOUR WALK WITH THE LORD.

Day 5

Luke 10:38-42

—

Practice this week's
memory verse
on page 145.

Overwhelm

The demands of motherhood can feel like too much at times. There is simply not enough time in the day to do everything we need to do. Throughout our days, we are expert boo-boo kissers (practically world-class doctors), dinner makers (basically gourmet chefs), and carpool drivers (virtually high-class chauffeurs). Not to mention the endless other hats we wear.

As moms, we also tend to place high expectations on ourselves. Think for a moment about all the requirements you place on yourself each day. Your day may include plans to:

> Meal plan, have a quiet time, cook breakfast, read to your children for thirty minutes, pack lunch, help with homework, drive to after-school activities, be involved with your children's ministry or youth group, make sure your child is doing well socially, do laundry, tackle a stained T-shirt, spend time with your husband, clean the bathrooms, maintain the budget, pay the bills, schedule a family game night, fill up the gas tank, cook dinner, give baths, clean the house, call a friend, do the bedtime routine...

The list above does not even include the expectations others may place on you, including your spouse, your children, your extended family, your neighbors, or your workplace. The constant demands for our time are enough to make anyone feel tired. The overwhelming busyness can easily lead to feelings of stress and panic.

But should we be this busy? Sometimes overwhelmingly busy seasons are necessities. Maybe, we are in a rare season of change, unable to find regular rhythms of rest. Unique life circumstances require an inordinate amount of attention from us. Yet often, our problem with busyness is self-inflicted. Our season of overwhelming busyness becomes a pattern. We overcommit, not wanting to disappoint others. We do not know how to say "no," and we think we need to do it all. We subconsciously believe that our child's salvation depends on the goodness of our parenting, and we over-parent, believing that our children's future is primarily in our hands, not the Lord's.

In today's Scripture reading, we are reminded of the importance of proper priorities through the story of Mary and Martha. As these two sisters both sought to do the right thing, Jesus reminded them of the better choice: to sit before the feet of Jesus and worship Him.

In Luke 10, Mary and Martha had visitors in their home. Wanting to be a good host, Martha rushed anxiously about her house, distracted with her many tasks (verse 40). But eventually, she became frustrated with her sister, who did not help her but instead sat before the feet of Jesus. Martha grew so bothered that she asked Jesus to intervene. But Jesus, out of love for Martha, did not send Mary into the kitchen to help her sister. Instead, he reoriented Martha's priorities. He said, "You are worried and upset about many things, but one thing is necessary. Mary has made the right choice, and it will not be taken away from her" (verses 41–42).

Sometimes in our mothering, our priorities can also become off-kilter. We fill our days to the brim with activities, but we forget the most important task of all: worshiping Jesus. We rush around trying to maintain and sustain our dream lives, and we forget to pause and commune with Christ.

Throughout the Gospels, Jesus is a perfect example of how to endure busy seasons while remaining faithful to God. While on earth, Jesus was constantly being pursued by people. Given His ability to heal and perform miracles, Jesus was regularly interrupted by people.

Maybe you can relate to His experience. Though you try to find rest, escaping into your bedroom for a minute of quiet, your children find you. They call for you every hour of the day. Jesus understands. He was a man who had no place to lay His head (Matthew 8:19–20) and who sacrificed comfort, quiet, and security for the sake of others. Even so, Jesus also found time to be alone and pray (Mark 1:35). He prioritized His relationship with the Father, even when His schedule was busy. Out of the overflow of His faith in God, He loved people and regularly endured tiredness for the sake of loving the lost.

Because of His humanity, Jesus did not visit every town and do every miracle. He disappointed people. Sick people were left unhealed. Hungry people went unfed. Yet Jesus perfectly fulfilled the Father's mission for Him. In the same way, faithfulness to the Lord will mean that we cannot do it all. We will need to say "no" to some responsibilities so that we can say "yes" to the most important ones. We must choose to fail in some areas so that we can succeed with our most important priorities. "Balance," if defined as doing all things perfectly, is not possible, but we are prioritizing properly when we place our faith in Christ.

If you are in a season of overwhelming busyness, prioritize your walk with the Lord. Thankfully, God has given us everything we need for life and godliness. He can help us reorient our priorities and simplify our schedules so that we can love God and our families well.

Not only this, but aim to depend on the Lord through even the most mundane tasks. Today's problem of overwhelming busyness might seem, at first glance, directly opposed to yesterday's emotion of laziness. But in actuality, they both present the same temptation. In laziness or busyness, we can be tempted to rely on ourselves rather than the Lord. While laziness may seek peace by avoiding issues, busyness seeks peace by controlling them. Yet through the gospel, Christ offers us another option. We can be faithful in the activities of today while constantly depending on Jesus and worshiping Him.

Even with the million demands of motherhood, Jesus reminds us that one thing is better today: to sit at His feet. Let us choose to prioritize this better option today.

"We will need to say 'no' to some responsibilities so that we can say 'yes' to the most important ones. We must choose to fail in some areas so that we can succeed with our most important priorities."

Day 5 Questions

Spend time praying through your calendar today. Is your busyness based on temporary, external reasons or self-inflicted choices? Does your calendar reflect biblical priorities?

Read Psalm 90 and 1 Peter 4:7–11. How would you like to live your life in light of eternity?

Complete the End-of-Week Reflection on the next page.

End-of-Week Reflection

Think back on all of the Scripture that you read and studied this week
as you answer the questions below.

What did you observe about God and His character?

What did you learn about the condition of mankind and yourself?

How did this week's Scripture point to the gospel?

How do the truths you have learned this week about God, man, and the gospel give you hope, peace, and encouragement?

How should you respond to what you read and learned this week? *Write down one or two specific action steps you can take this week to apply what you learned. Then, write a prayer in response to your study of God's Word.*

Week 4 Application

Before we begin a new week of study, take some time to apply
and share the truths of Scripture you learned this week.
Here are a few ideas of how you could do this:

 ### Meet Up

Schedule a meet-up with a friend to share what you are learning
from God's Word.

 ### Worship

Spend time worshiping God in a way that is meaningful to you, whether that is
taking a walk in nature, painting, drawing, singing, etc.

 ### Pray

Use these prompts to journal or pray through what God is revealing to you
through your study of His Word.

- *Lord, I feel . . .*

- *Lord, You are . . .*

- *Lord, forgive me for . . .*

- *Lord, help me with . . .*

Paraphrase

Paraphrase the Scripture you read this week.

 Dig Deeper

Use a study Bible or commentary to help you answer questions that came up as you read this week's Scripture.

 Take Action

Take steps to fulfill the action steps you listed on Day 5.

 Highlight

Use highlighters to mark the places you see the metanarrative of Scripture in one or more of the passages that you read this week. (See "The Metanarrative of Scripture" on page 15.)

"Remember, loving your children is not based on emotion. Rather, it is your responsibility to pour yourself into your child's life so that he or she grows up to love Christ."

John F. MacArthur Jr.

(MACARTHUR 2011)

God's Grace is Sufficient for Motherhood

Week 5 Introduction

During our final week together, we will remember what we have learned about God's compassion for us. Motherhood can be hard, but thankfully, there is hope for us even on our difficult days. When we are at the end of our ropes, unsure how to respond to the newest set of mothering decisions, we are never truly alone. God is always with us to guide us and to help us. And even when our weeks do not go according to our plans, Jesus always guides our steps. Even though we are consistently challenged and pushed beyond our natural abilities — though our patience is tested and our limitedness is exposed — God is enough for us.

This week, we will specifically focus on the following reminders:

Motherhood is a beautiful and important work.	God is with us always, even through the unseen and stressful moments of motherhood.	Jesus is coming again. One day, He will make all things right.

As we finish this study, pray that you will run to the Lord in every emotion. Pray that you will turn to the Lord and remain consistent in His Word even after this study ends, loving the Lord through Bible study and in prayer. Reflect also on the following questions before starting the final week of this study:

How have you seen the Lord grow your love for His Word through this study?	In what ways have you experienced Jesus in the trenches with you in motherhood?	How does the hope of heaven encourage you on the hard days?

MEMORY VERSE

Psalm 90:12

Teach us to number our days
carefully so that we may develop
wisdom in our hearts.

AS MOMS, WE CALL
OUT TO A GOD WHO IS
LIMITLESS IN ENERGY,
WISDOM, AND POWER.

Count the Days (They Are Limited)

There is a popular phrase in mothering that says, "The days are long, but the years are short." This advice is often passed down from older, empty-nest women to younger, struggling moms. With good intentions, older women desire to help younger moms savor the hard moments of parenting. But sometimes, this advice falls flat in the midst of our long days. The encouragement to "savor the days" does not feel particularly helpful when we are gasping for air, struggling to steal moments of quiet away from our children and locking ourselves in the pantry. We think, *The years may be short, but today feels too long. How am I going to make it to bedtime?*

Are you in a season of the "long days" of mothering? Though you love your children more than life itself, do you look longingly to the simpler days of your younger years? Or maybe, you cannot wait for the next season of life—for the diapers to end, for school to begin, or for your child to start driving. You regularly look forward at what is to come or backward at what was before, rarely enjoying the current moment of mothering itself.

Or perhaps, your story is the opposite. You are currently enjoying your season of mothering without any sense of urgency. You soak up the mild inconveniences of motherhood with supreme joy out of an abundance of love for your children. But in your mothering, you tend to leave the hard moments of parenting for "later." After all, you do not want to disrupt these joyful moments of playing with a stern word of discipline. You can do that tomorrow. Your time as a mom feels vast and limitless.

In every season, Psalm 90 is a helpful reminder for us. Psalm 90 is the oldest psalm of Moses and was written when the Israelites were wandering in the wilderness (Platt 2020, 358). As the people waited on the promises of the Lord, Moses prayed for God's favor. He reflected on life through an eternal perspective and looked to the Lord for purpose, satisfaction, and hope (verses 13–17).

The truths of Psalm 90 can encourage us in our mothering today as we also remember two fundamental truths that change and direct our lives: God is eternal, and we are not.

God is eternal. As Moses wrote, the Lord has been our refuge in every generation (verse 1). From the age of the Israelites wandering in the desert to your present season of life, God has always been a safe space for His people. In every generation—from the simpler days of our grandmothers to the technology-filled lives of new moms—God is our fortress. Before the world was even created, He was God, from eternity to eternity (verse 2). And because God is eternal, He has an eternal perspective. We do not understand time from God's perspective because a thousand years are like yesterday in God's sight (verse 4). Yet the Lord lives in realms of eternal wisdom with understanding lightyears beyond our own. As moms, we call out to a God who is limitless in energy, wisdom, and power. He is eternal.

Though God is eternal, we are not. While our God lives forever, working with unbounded energy, we return to dust (verse 3). We are like grass that comes and goes, flourishing one day and withering the next. Our days are limited, lasting perhaps seventy or eighty years, and each year is filled with struggle and sorrow (verse 10).

In light of this frailty, Moses prayed, "Teach us to number our days carefully so that we may develop wisdom in our hearts" (verse 12). As moms, that means that while the days feel long, they are limited. Every one of our days is

counted, and our moments of stressful mothering will end. The number of times our children will cry for us in the night is limited. The number of first days of school is limited, and the number of times they will ask for "one more book" is limited. The years our children will live in our home are numbered.

Sometimes, we will notice when these seasons of motherhood change, rejoicing when the years of diapers, bottles, or sippy cups finally cease. Other times, the seasons will pass away slowly and silently, vanishing without a trace. Months later, we realize that we have not been called "Mommy" in a while. We are now simply "Mom." We did not recognize the day our names changed, just as we did not know which would be the last bedtime song we would sing. The season changed as quickly and unpredictably as the withering grass of Psalm 90.

Because these earthly mothering days are known and counted by God, every single one matters. God has given us the unique opportunity to live today with intentionality, recognizing that He leads our steps. Therefore, let us be faithful to make the most of these numbered days of discipleship. We are not guaranteed tomorrow, but we have the opportunity to cherish and teach our children about God today. As the nineteenth-century pastor Charles Spurgeon said, "Let us recognize the true value of children, and then we won't keep them back, but we shall be eager to lead them to Jesus at once" (Spurgeon 2018). In light of eternity, we can be satisfied in God as we joyfully lead our children to the Savior (verse 14).

As it turns out, there is wisdom in the old adage, "The days are long, but the years are short." As we count the days of our motherhood, we know they are numbered (verse 12). We have the greatest gift of pointing our children to the Lord in these very short years. And at the same time, when the days feel long, we know: they are limited too. His grace is sufficient for each day.

"God has given us the unique opportunity to live today with intentionality, recognizing that He leads our steps. Therefore, let us be faithful to make the most of these numbered days of discipleship."

Day 1 Questions

Is there a parenting responsibility that you have neglected or postponed, assuming that you can do it tomorrow? How can you be faithful in what God has called you to today?

Read Isaiah 57:15. How does the eternal nature of God bring you comfort today?

Spend time praying for your children today. Pray for their salvation, their character, their friends, and their lives in light of eternity.

Today's Notes

ATTRIBUTE OF GOD I AM MEDITATING ON TODAY:

REMEMBER THIS:

WE ARE NOT
PERFECT MOMS, BUT
GOD'S GRACE IS
ENOUGH FOR US.

Day 2

Colossians 1:28-29
Colossians 3:23-24
1 Corinthians 15:10

—

Practice this week's
memory verse
on page 185.

The Important Work of Mothering (Your Work Matters)

Do you feel unseen in your mothering? Maybe as you rise up early in the morning to prepare for the day, you feel alone. No one thanks you for the meals you make each night or the fights you break up in the car. No one thinks twice about the clothes bought, the lunch boxes packed, and the prayers prayed. No one, it seems, sees all the sacrifices you make each day for your children.

In light of this, it is easy to wonder, *Does any of it even matter?* Does it matter when we press into the difficult moments of discipling our children, or can we ignore them? Does it matter if we are on our phones in front of our kids or if we read them the Bible? Does it matter if we dig into the Scriptures to see what they say about our difficult emotions? If no one even notices, does any of it matter?

While it is true that many of our mothering duties go unnoticed by our families, that does not mean that they are unseen. God sees everything. He sees every deed, knows every thought, and hears every prayer. He knows the exact number of times you have sung bedtime songs and how many nighttime stories you have read. He knows the precise number of milliseconds you have been awake in the night because of a crying baby, a bad dream, or a child's stomach bug. He knows the number of lunches you have made and the number of times you have helped with homework. God knows and sees it all.

God knows every joy you have experienced as well. He knows the moments when your heart seems to grow and warm—when your child takes her first step, when she says, "I love you" for the first time, and when he makes you laugh. The Lord is with you even then, sustaining and cherishing each moment with you. He is there in every good moment and in every difficult one.

So when we feel alone, as if our service as moms is insignificant, we can look to Scripture to remember: the Lord cares. But not only this, as Paul reminds us in today's verses: our work matters because it matters to God. Whether we are wiping down tables or helping with SAT prep, God calls us to work hard for His glory, remembering that we work for the Lord, not for the appreciation of our families. Our reward and our inheritance come from Him (Colossians 3:23–24).

Like Paul's ministry to the Church, much of our ministry to our children does not yield immediate fruit. The work of mothering and the daily discipleship of our children is a long-term investment. Each day, we plant seeds in the lives of our children. We toil and work, not for immediate gratification or instant change but for their eternal good. Even so, our daily laboring and our hard work in motherhood are not meaningless. Our gentle responses to the angering situations of our days are not insignificant. Every loving and godly response is a part of our gospel work as we strive with all God's strength that works so powerfully within us.

In the same way that Paul worked with all his energy for the gospel, we also can work hard for the gospel within our spheres of influence. We can proclaim Jesus within our homes, warning and teaching our children with all wisdom, so that we can present them mature in Christ (Colossians 1:28–29). We can work hard in our mothering for God's glory and by the grace that is at work within us (1 Corinthians 15:10). And as we work, God will help us to fulfill His plans for us each day.

At the same time, as we all have experienced, we will fall short in our mothering. Even with the best intentions, we will indulge in sinful impulses, respond with anger, and give in to sinful fear. We are not perfect moms, but God's grace is enough for us. He not only forgives us but also helps us change.

By the grace of God, we are not who we were (1 Corinthians 15:9–10, 2 Corinthians 5:17). Throughout our spiritual lives, the Lord has been growing us and transforming us to look more like Him. And when we fall short, we can repent of our sins and rest in the grace of Christ, knowing that the Lord will continue His work in us.

In light of this, spend a moment now to reflect: How has God worked in your life through this study? More specifically, how have you seen growth in your mothering throughout this study? Maybe throughout this study, you have felt convicted of a specific sin and have run to God for grace. Maybe you have repented to the Lord and said, "I'm sorry" to your children for the first time, admitting that you have done something wrong. Maybe you have started to actively pursue the things of God through difficult emotions, aiming to lead your children in the faith. In any case, by God's grace, you are not where you were. He has given you a grand and beautiful responsibility in motherhood to love and care for your children, and He is growing you as you work in this role.

So in summary, does your mothering matter? Without question. Every late-night, tear-stained, coffee-filled moment matters to the Lord. Your work matters. Every peanut butter and jelly sandwich you make, every uniform you iron, every diaper you change, every runny nose you wipe matters to the Lord. The Lord sees every single sacrifice. You matter to Him.

Let us, then, work hard in the important work of mothering by the grace of God. God has chosen you to be "mom" to your specific children, and He will use your gospel work for good, according to His mysterious and perfect plan.

"We can work hard in our mothering for God's glory and by the grace that is at work within us (1 Corinthians 15:10). And as we work, God will help us to fulfill His plans for us each day."

Day 2 Questions

Do you regularly feel unnoticed in your mothering? How does today's Scripture encourage you when you feel alone?

Read 1 Corinthians 10:31. What would it look like for you to work for the glory of God as you parent?

How is mothering the "long game?" How does keeping an eternal perspective change the way you view the day-to-day moments of motherhood?

Today's Notes

ATTRIBUTE OF GOD I AM MEDITATING ON TODAY:

REMEMBER THIS:

THE DAILY STRESSES
OF MOTHERHOOD
ARE REAL, BUT
SO IS GOD'S GRACE.

Day 3

2 Corinthians 12:9
2 Timothy 4:16–18

—

Practice this week's
memory verse
on page 185.

In Every Daily Stress, His Grace is Sufficient

"Mom, will you play with me?"
"Mom, she hit me!"
"Mom, I failed my math test."
"Mom, can I go to Stacey's party this weekend?"

How many times do your children call your name each day? You may feel your blood pressure rising with each call, knowing that each call requires you to make a decision: Should you play with your child now or start to cook dinner? What is the proper discipline strategy for a hitting child, after all? Can your child go to Stacey's party or not? There are many stressful and instantaneous choices that we make each day as moms. On top of that, we also juggle the normal pressure of motherhood: carpooling, managing after-school activities, navigating sibling rivalries, and taming messy houses.

When we feel stressed, we naturally run to sources of relief. Sometimes, we throw ourselves into our work, seeking validation from the approval of others in the workplace. Other times, we try to escape, deep diving into the world of television documentaries or personal hobbies. Occasionally, we even avoid our children. There are plenty of opportunities in the world to avoid our mothering responsibilities and alleviate stress. But how does Christ want us to respond to stressful situations?

To answer that question, let us consider what we have learned throughout the past several weeks. Throughout this study, we have discussed a number of difficult emotions that come with mothering. We have talked about how we are regularly tempted toward discouragement, self-pity, and anxiety. We have discussed our anger and impatience in mothering. And we have also learned that no matter the emotion, the answer is not to buy a better planner or sign up for more activities with our children. The path to peace in the midst of stressful situations is not found in any circumstantial change. It is not even hidden in our own capacities or abilities. True contentment, joy, and peace are only possible in Jesus.

As we also read in today's verses, stress is not an experience unique to moms. The gospel worker Paul endured much stress throughout his ministry. But even when he was alone and deserted by everyone, he found strength and encouragement in the Lord (2 Timothy 4:16–17). He was rescued from every evil work and brought safely into God's heavenly kingdom (verse 18). As a result, Paul gave glory and praise to God (verse 18).

Similarly, in the midst of our difficulties of ministering as moms, our hope is found in Christ alone. Even when we feel alone, abandoned, and deserted by everyone, God is with us to strengthen and encourage us. When the difficult emotions of mothering paralyze us, we can cry out to the Lord, knowing that He is our help.

So if you feel stressed or impatient today, turn to Jesus. He can use every moment of unplanned, patience-testing trouble for His glory and your good (Romans 8:28). He wants you to grow in patience as a mom, and He will help you. By the Spirit's work, you can grow in self-control, relying on the patience that God supplies and repenting of your lack of patience. He is your very present help in times of need (Psalm 46:1).

If you feel nervous, strained, or depleted today,

run to Christ. Even when life feels empty, there is always hope in Jesus. Although it can feel tempting to isolate in our darkness, God longs to bring you hope and peace. He is the life-giver, the One who brings hope to the hopeless. He will provide for you, and His goodness never ends.

If you feel pressured and overwhelmed by your never-ending to-do list, fall to Jesus, who perfectly endured stress. Take a deep breath, and remember that Christ lived a perfect life on our behalf. He perfectly fulfilled every "to-do" of the Father; we cannot. Throughout His life, Jesus faced impossibly hard days, yet He did not sin. He endured in love, even when He was tired. He never grew sinfully angry or selfish. He never gave up on His children. And now, He credits His perfection to us. We are washed clean of our sins and counted as righteous because of the perfection of Jesus.

When we remember Jesus in the midst of our stressful days, this practice helps to reorient our narratives and identities as moms. As Kira Nelson, a writer at The Gospel Coalition, said, "Our success or sacrifice in motherhood shouldn't be what defines our narrative. What ought to captivate our hearts and minds is a story—one not ultimately about us but about Christ our Redeemer. As a Christian, I need to understand I'm not the hero or the center of my story. The saddest part of my story isn't that I'm overwhelmed, taken for granted, and spit up on. The saddest part of my story is that I was dead in my sins. The climax of my story isn't how I overcame challenges so my child could graduate with honors. The climax of my story is that my Savior was obedient to the point of death to ransom a people for himself" (2023).

As Christian women, we know that Jesus is the hero of our story, our Redeemer and Savior. He is our anchor on stressful days. He has dealt with our greatest problems on the cross, setting us free from sin and death and offering us new life. Surely, He will help us in these smaller moments of stressful mothering too.

The daily stresses of motherhood are real, but so is God's grace. He is our hero and all that we need.

"Even when we feel alone, abandoned, and deserted by everyone, God is with us to strengthen and encourage us. When the difficult emotions of mothering paralyze us, we can cry out to the Lord, knowing that He is our help."

Day 3 Questions

How have you grown in your response to stressful situations over the past five weeks?

Read Psalm 94:18-19. What would it look like for you to cry out to the Lord in the midst of your stress today?

Share something that you learned today with another mom. Ask how you can pray for her in the midst of her stressful days of mothering.

Today's Notes

ATTRIBUTE OF GOD I AM MEDITATING ON TODAY:

REMEMBER THIS:

"Ask, and it will be given to you.
Seek, and you will find.
Knock, and the door will be
opened to you.
For everyone who asks receives,
and the one who seeks finds,
and to the one who knocks,
the door will be opened.
Who among you, if his son asks
him for bread, will give him a stone?
Or if he asks for a fish,
will give him a snake?
If you then, who are evil,
know how to give good gifts
to your children,
how much more will your
Father in heaven give good things
to those who ask him."

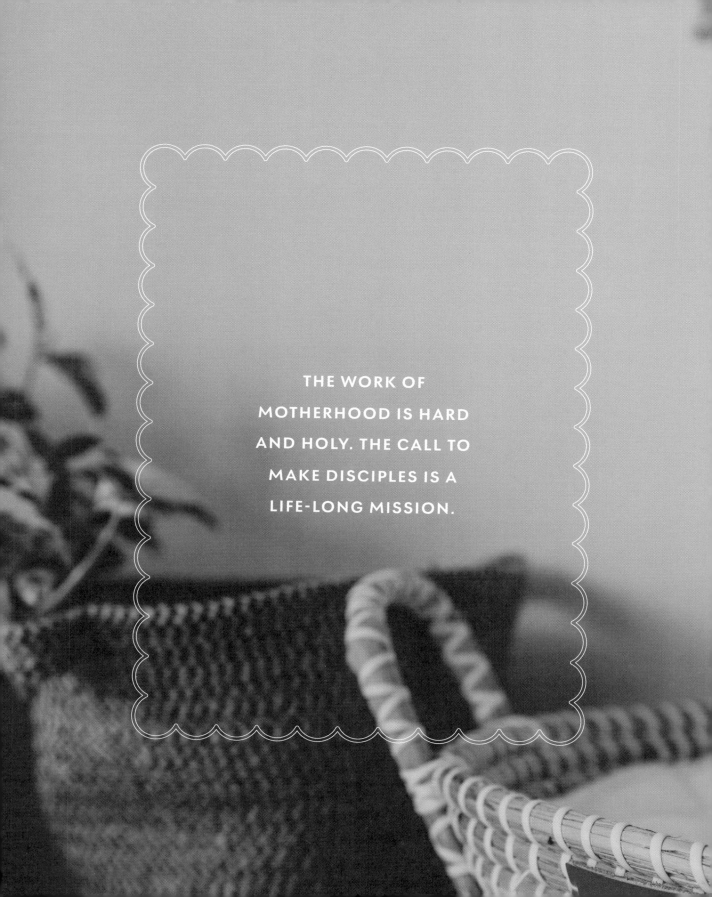

THE WORK OF
MOTHERHOOD IS HARD
AND HOLY. THE CALL TO
MAKE DISCIPLES IS A
LIFE-LONG MISSION.

Day 4

Matthew 28:18-20
2 Timothy 1:1-5

—

Practice this week's
memory verse
on page 185.

Jesus Is with Us in the Trenches

In *The Pilgrim's Progress*, John Bunyan describes the journey of a man named Christian. Throughout this allegorical narrative, Christian faces many troubles on his way to the heavenly Celestial City. Even after Christian places his faith in Jesus, he endures challenges, temptations, and persecution. He walks through the Valley of Humiliation and faces danger in the city of Vanity. He spends time at the Doubting Castle and is kept in prison by its owner, Great Despair. Even so, Christian endures to the end, joyfully making his way to his eternal home.

In the same way, we also labor on as Christians toward our heavenly home. Even after we place our faith in Christ, we still face troubles. We serve God with broken bodies and frail dispositions. We fall short. We face daily challenges, temptations, and trouble. But throughout it all, Jesus is with us. He is with us in the trenches of life, and He calls us to a great mission with Him. He will sustain us until the end.

While on this great heavenly journey, God has given us an important mission: to make disciples. We read of this mission in Matthew 28:18–20 before Jesus ascended into heaven. Jesus gave this command after enduring a grueling death on the cross, bearing our guilt and shame. Following His resurrection, Jesus appeared to His disciples and gave them a series of final instructions. One of His commands was this: to "go . . . and make disciples of all nations, baptizing them in the name of the Father and of the Son and of the Holy Spirit" (verse 19).

Just as Jesus told His disciples to "go," He calls us to go too. We are called to go outside of our comfort zones, outside of our routines, and sometimes even outside our passport countries to share the good news of Jesus. And as moms, we are called to go to our children and teach them about God. We are to teach our children all that God has commanded, remembering that He will be with us until the end of the age (verse 20).

In our motherhood, God has given us an important mission: the ministry of reconciliation (2 Corinthians 5:18). This means that we have a greater responsibility than simply making sure our children eat enough vegetables (as important as veggies are for our kids). We have the incredible opportunity to point our children toward the beauty of their Creator, encouraging them in word and deed to be reconciled to God. God calls us to make disciples. Let us start this very important mission by making disciples within our families.

Yet often, we fall short of this command. We prioritize swim practice and piano lessons over family discipleship moments. Whether through our words or actions, we teach our children that sports matter more than church—that our greatest treasure is not Jesus but what we do or what we own. Even worse, we do not grieve our lack of godly leadership, whether resulting from physical exhaustion or spiritual apathy. But thankfully, there is hope for us when we fall short. When we fail, neglecting our godly responsibilities through willful disobedience or human limitations, Christ meets us where we are. He is with us in the battle, both to forgive us when we fall short and to equip us for this great responsibility.

As we grow closer to God and aim to make spiritual discipleship a priority, God can change our hearts and priorities. Family worship can change from something we dread to something we look forward to. Author Joel Beeke said, "Family worship is invaluable. For the last 17 years of my life, I can say to you that family worship time is the most important thing I do in my life. I wouldn't miss it for anything in the world. It's the highlight of my day. It doesn't mean it always goes perfect and it doesn't mean it even always goes well, but I know and I feel to the core of my being that it is critical to have family worship" (2011).

Through our daily discipleship, God can bless our investment in our children in ways we never thought possible. One example of this is seen in the life of Timothy (2 Timothy 1:1–5). Interestingly, Timothy was a gospel worker who was greatly influenced by two women in his life, his grandmother Lois and his mother Eunice. His father was likely not a believer, but these women had a great influence on him, teaching him about the Lord. Yet even as they patiently taught young Timothy about the gospel, they never could have dreamed that God would use him to bring so many to the faith or that their names would be included in the Bible for all eternity.

Lois and Eunice were not perfect women, nor did they perfectly teach Timothy about God. But the Lord blessed their daily discipleship of Timothy in ways they never could have imagined. Similarly, while we may not see the immediate fruit of our discipleship in our homes, we know that God will bless our faith and reward our obedience. He is not a stingy God. He is generous and works in greater and grander ways than we could ever imagine.

Just as the pilgrim, Christian, was distracted on his path to the Celestial City, we too can easily become distracted from our mission by the fleeting pleasures of this world. But as we parent, let us keep in mind our eternal destination, prioritizing the spiritual development of our children over their athletic and scholastic achievements. These are the moments of eternal significance.

The work of motherhood is hard and holy. The call to make disciples is a life-long mission. But Jesus is with us on this journey. He will lead us on until we reach our eternal home.

"As moms, we are called to go to our children and teach them about God. We are to teach our children all that God has commanded, remembering that He will be with us until the end of the age."

Day 4 Questions

Read Isaiah 49:5-6 in light of today's passages. What does this teach you about God's heart and desire for the salvation of the world?

How have you discipled your children over the past few months? What would you like to change or add? For ideas in discipling your children, see page 124.

Reflecting on the last five weeks, which day was most helpful to you? Share something you learned from that study day with your children.

Today's Notes

ATTRIBUTE OF GOD I AM MEDITATING ON TODAY:

REMEMBER THIS:

CHRIST WILL HOLD
YOU FAST THROUGH
YOUR DIFFICULT MOMENTS
OF MOTHERING.

Day 5

Revelation 21:1-7

—

Practice this week's
memory verse
on page 185.

Labor Pains: He Is Coming Again

As we wrap up this study, we want to say: Great job! You did it. In the midst of your challenging season of motherhood, you prioritized being with the Lord and being in His Word. The time you spent studying the Bible will not return void. Your hours spent in prayer and study over the past several weeks will be a gift, not only for your own faith but also for your children.

Most moms wish they had an older woman who could give them a hug, offer them free childcare, and tell them they are doing a great job. And although we cannot be there physically to offer spontaneous childcare or give tangible hugs, we are cheering you on! Well done, friend.

As we finish this study, we want to spend one final day looking forward to our eternal hope, eagerly anticipating the day when Jesus will return and all will be right. As we read in Revelation 21, there is a day coming when every minor inconvenience and every strenuous pain will be no more. We will finally be with God. He will live with us (verse 3), and our pain will be no more (verse 4). He will comfort us and wipe every tear from our eyes (verse 4). Every tear, pressure, and moment of anxiety will be no more. Discomfort, stress, and sin will be removed because Jesus will make all things new (verses 4–5).

This means that although we currently labor on, faithfully working in our mothering ministry, these moments will end. One day, we will see Jesus face-to-face (Revelation 22:3–4). Our seemingly endless days of motherhood laboring will finally make sense when we see Him. We will give praise to the Alpha and the Omega, the beginning and end, erupting in worship to the One who offers the water of life to the thirsty (Revelation 21:6). He alone is worthy of our attention, worship, and praise. And He is with us as we labor on, calling us His sons and daughters (verse 7).

The hymn "He Will Hold Me Fast" was originally written by Ada R. Habershon and later adapted by Keith and Kristyn Getty. It reminds us of this day to come while recognizing our need for Jesus through our current, daily struggles. As the hymn says, Christ will not only hold us fast, sustaining us through today's troubles, but He will also raise us to new life in Him. Read the lyrics below (or better yet, find an online version to listen as you read):

> When I fear my faith will fail,
> Christ will hold me fast;
> When the tempter would prevail,
> He will hold me fast.
> I could never keep my hold
> Through life's fearful path;
> For my love is often cold;
> He must hold me fast.
> Those He saves are His delight,
> Christ will hold me fast;
> Precious in His holy sight,
> He will hold me fast.
> He'll not let my soul be lost;
> His promises shall last;
> Bought by Him at such a cost,
> He will hold me fast.
> For my life He bled and died,
> Christ will hold me fast;
> Justice has been satisfied;
> He will hold me fast.
> Raised with Him to endless life,
> He will hold me fast
> 'Til our faith is turned to sight
> When He comes at last!

Christ will hold you fast through your difficult moments of mothering. So as you press on through your long, hard mothering days, look to Jesus. He walks with you, and He is coming again to mend every weary bone and heal every bruised heart. You can cling to Christ in seasons of sorrow and in seasons of joy, knowing that He leads you to the Tree of Life (Revelation 22:14).

As you look to Jesus, continue also to invest in the ordinary means of grace that God has given you: prayer, church, and reading the Word. God has given us these gifts for a healthy Christian life, and they are essential for your spiritual flourishing.

Finally, as we close, one final reminder: God is our greatest treasure. Our greatest goal in life is not to have emotionally easy mothering days. Our goal is to worship Christ. Whether or not we feel successful as moms, and whether or not our children are behaving well at any particular moment, we can still be joyful and content in Jesus because He has given us everything that we need in Himself. As pastor David Mathis explains, "It is almost too good to be true that God not only *saves us* from the eternal punishment we deserve for our sin, but he also *satisfies us* forever with himself. And this is the very joy for which we were made. God is not the cosmic killjoy many of us may have feared in our youth. Rather, he is the God who, in Christ, stretches out his arms to us, saying, 'Come, all who are thirsty!'" (Mathis 2019).

Jesus is our greatest joy and our constant friend. He will hold us fast. Every day, whether weary or joyful, let us drink in the riches of His grace.

May God bless your family as you treasure Christ together.

"May the LORD bless you and protect you; may the LORD make his face shine on you and be gracious to you; may the LORD look with favor on you and give you peace."

NUMBERS 6:24-26

Day 5 Questions

Read John 14:1-4. How does the reminder that Jesus is coming again help you on the hard days of motherhood?

How would you like to live differently in light of this study? Choose one or two specific areas of personal application that you would like to focus on.

Complete the End-of-Week Reflection on the next page.

End-of-Week Reflection

Think back on all of the Scripture that you read and studied this week as you answer the questions below.

What did you observe about God and His character?

What did you learn about the condition of mankind and yourself?

How did this week's Scripture point to the gospel?

How do the truths you have learned this week about God, man, and the gospel give you hope, peace, and encouragement?

How should you respond to what you read and learned this week? *Write down one or two specific action steps you can take this week to apply what you learned. Then, write a prayer in response to your study of God's Word.*

Week 5 Application

As this last week of study comes to an end, take some time to apply and share the truths of Scripture you learned this week. Here are a few ideas of how you could do this:

Meet Up

Schedule a meet-up with a friend to share what you are learning from God's Word.

Worship

Spend time worshiping God in a way that is meaningful to you, whether that is taking a walk in nature, painting, drawing, singing, etc.

Pray

Use these prompts to journal or pray through what God is revealing to you through your study of His Word.

- *Lord, I feel . . .*

- *Lord, You are . . .*

- *Lord, forgive me for . . .*

- *Lord, help me with . . .*

Paraphrase

Paraphrase the Scripture you read this week.

Dig Deeper

Use a study Bible or commentary to help you answer questions that came up as you read this week's Scripture.

Take Action

Take steps to fulfill the action steps you listed on Day 5.

Highlight

Use highlighters to mark the places you see the metanarrative of Scripture in one or more of the passages that you read this week. (See "The Metanarrative of Scripture" on page 15.)

What is the Gospel?

Thank you for reading and enjoying this study with us! We are abundantly grateful for the Word of God, the instruction we glean from it, and the ever-growing understanding it provides for us of God's character. We are also thankful that Scripture continually points to one thing in innumerable ways: the gospel.

We remember our brokenness when we read about the fall of Adam and Eve in the garden of Eden (Genesis 3), where sin entered into a perfect world and maimed it. We remember the necessity that something innocent must die to pay for our sin when we read about the atoning sacrifices in the Old Testament. We read that we have all sinned and fallen short of the glory of God (Romans 3:23) and that the penalty for our brokenness, the wages of our sin, is death (Romans 6:23). We all need grace and mercy, but most importantly, we all need a Savior.

We consider the goodness of God when we realize that He did not plan to leave us in this dire state. We see His promise to buy us back from the clutches of sin and death in Genesis 3:15. And we see that promise accomplished with Jesus Christ on the cross. Jesus Christ knew no sin yet became sin so that we might become righteous through His sacrifice (2 Corinthians 5:21). Jesus was tempted in every way that we are and lived sinlessly. He was reviled yet still yielded Himself for our sake, that we may have life abundant in Him. Jesus lived the perfect life that we could not live and died the death that we deserved.

The gospel is profound yet simple. There are many mysteries in it that we will never understand this side of heaven, but there is still overwhelming weight to its implications in this life. The gospel tells of our sinfulness and God's goodness and a gracious gift that compels a response. We are saved by grace through faith, which means that we rest with faith in the grace that Jesus Christ displayed on the cross (Ephesians 2:8–9). We cannot save ourselves from our brokenness or do any amount of good works to merit God's favor. Still, we can have faith that what Jesus accomplished in His death, burial, and resurrection was more than enough for our salvation and our eternal delight. When we accept God, we are commanded to die to ourselves and our sinful desires and live a life worthy of the calling we have received (Ephesians 4:1). The gospel compels us to be sanctified, and in so doing, we are conformed to the likeness of Christ Himself. This is hope. This is redemption. This is the gospel.

GENESIS 3:15

I will put hostility between you and the woman, and between your offspring and her offspring. He will strike your head, and you will strike his heel.

ROMANS 3:23

For all have sinned and fall short of the glory of God.

ROMANS 6:23

For the wages of sin is death, but the gift of God is eternal life in Christ Jesus our Lord.

2 CORINTHIANS 5:21

He made the one who did not know sin to be sin for us, so that in him we might become the righteousness of God.

EPHESIANS 2:8–9

For you are saved by grace through faith, and this is not from yourselves; it is God's gift—not from works, so that no one can boast.

EPHESIANS 4:1–3

Therefore I, the prisoner in the Lord, urge you to walk worthy of the calling you have received, with all humility and gentleness, with patience, bearing with one another in love, making every effort to keep the unity of the Spirit through the bond of peace.

BIBLIOGRAPHY

Adams, Jay E. *1 Corinthians and II Corinthians*. Cordova, TN: Institute for Nouthetic Studies, 2020.

Akin, Daniel L., et al. *Exalting Jesus in Psalms 101–150*. Nashville, TN: B&H Publishing Group, 2021.

Bancroft, Eric. "Anxiety: When I Feel Like I Am Losing Control." Sermon. Grace Church. June 05, 2021. Miami Shores, FL. YouTube video, 55:06. https://www.youtube.com/watch?v=MRJa8oDIR5c.

Bancroft, Eric. "Say 'Good Bye' to Alka-Seltzer: Turning Worry into Worship." Sermon. Grace Church. March 15, 2020. Miami Shores, FL. YouTube video, 43:19. https://www.youtube.com/watch?v=RAOu8i0Y2wU.

Barnett, Paul. *The Message of 2 Corinthians: Power in Weakness*. England: InterVarsity Press, 1988.

Beeke, Joel. "Leading Family Worship." *Desiring God*. February 2, 2011. https://www.desiringgod.org/messages/leading-family-worship.

Begg, Alistair. *Truth for Life: 365 Daily Devotions*. The Good Book Company, 2001.

Brockman, Rob. "What is the Difference Between Grumbling and Lament?" *The Gospel Coalition*. June 6, 2022. https://ca.thegospelcoalition.org/article/what-is-the-difference-between-grumbling-and-lament/.

Bunyan, John. *The Pilgrim's Progress*. Penguin Classics, January 27, 2009.

Clarkson, Sally. *Own Your Life: Living with Deep Intention, Bold Faith, and Generous Love*. Tyndale Momentum, 2015.

Clarkson, Sally and Sarah Mae. *Desperate: Hope for the Mom Who Needs to Breathe*. Nashville, TN: Thomas Nelson, 2013.

Ferguson, Sinclair. *A Heart for God*. Carlisle, PA: Banner of Truth, 1987.

Getty, Keith and Kristyn. *He Will Hold Me Fast.* http://www.songlyrics.com/keith-kristyn-getty/he-will-hold-me-fast-lyrics/.

Groves, Alasdair. "Help! I Keep Losing My Temper." *Christian Counseling and Educational Foundation.* March 19, 2019. https://www.ccef.org/help-i-keep-losing-my-temper/.

Keller, Tim. *Paul's Letter to the Galatians: Leaders Guide.* New York: Redeemer Presbyterian Church, 2003.

Lowe, Julie. "The Danger of Comparison." *Christian Counseling and Educational Foundation.* January 5, 2022. https://www.ccef.org/the-danger-of-comparison/.

MacArthur, John F. *Divine Design: God's Complementary Roles for Men and Women.* Colorado Springs, CO: David C. Cook, 2011.

Mathis, David. "How to Seek Your Joy in God: Three Habits For Christian Hedonists." *Desiring God.* October 25, 2019. https://www.desiringgod.org/articles/how-to-seek-your-joy-in-god.

Moore, Beverly. "The Illusion of Control." *The Biblical Counseling Coalition.* February 2, 2018. https://www.biblicalcounselingcoalition.org/2018/02/02/the-illusion-of-control/.

Nelson, Kira. "Mothering Isn't Martyrdom." *The Gospel Coalition.* June 21, 2023. https://www.thegospelcoalition.org/article/motherhood-martyrdom/.

Osborne, Grant R. *Ephesians: Verse by Verse.* Bellingham, WA: Lexham Press, 2017.

Platt, David, Jim Shaddix, and Matt Mason. *Christ-Centered Exposition: Exalting Jesus in Psalm 51-100.* Nashville, TN: B&H Publishing Group, 2020.

Smith, J. Josh, and Daniel L. Akin. *Exalting Jesus in Psalms 1–50.* Nashville, TN: B&H Publishing Group, 2022.

Spafford, Horatio G. "It Is Well with My Soul." In *Hymns to the Living God.* Edited by Scott Aniol. 214. Fort Worth: Religious Affections Ministries, 2017. https://hymnary.org/hymn/HTLG2017/214.

Sproul, R.C. *Family Practice: God's Prescription for a Healthy Home*. Phillipsburg, NJ: P&R Publishing, 2001.

Spurgeon, Charles. *Come Ye Children: Obtaining Our Lord's Heart for Loving and Teaching Children*. Life Sentence Publishing, 2018.

Tripp, Paul David. November 3, 2016. Crossway. Facebook Video, 2:08. https://www.facebook.com/watch/?v=10154608547353632.

Tripp, Paul David. *Parenting: 14 Gospel Principles that Can Really Change Your Family*. Wheaton, IL: Crossway, 2016.

Warner, Anna Bartlett. *Jesus Loves Me, This I Know*. 1859.

Wilkin, Jen. "Do I Love My Kids Too Much?" *The Gospel Coalition*. August 29, 2016. https://www.thegospelcoalition.org/article/empty-nests-christian-mommy-guilt-misplaced-identity/.

Thank you for studying
God's Word with us!

CONNECT WITH US
@thedailygraceco
@dailygracepodcast

CONTACT US
info@thedailygraceco.com

SHARE
#thedailygraceco

VISIT US ONLINE
www.thedailygraceco.com

MORE DAILY GRACE
Daily Grace® Podcast